W9-BDN-000

1/13

3 1489 00640 5110

#31.93

FOOD
THE NEW GOLD

KATHLYN GAY

TWENTY-FIRST CENTURY BOOKS
MINNEAPOLIS

FREEPORT MEMORIAL LIBRARY

TO ALL THOSE CONSUMERS WHO
CAREFULLY CONSIDER WHAT
FOOD THEY BUY, WHERE THEY
BUY IT, AND THE ENVIRONMENTAL,
SOCIAL, AND HEALTH IMPACTS
OF THEIR CHOICES.
—K.G.

Copyright © 2013 by Kathlyn Gay

All rights reserved. International copyright secured. No part
of this book may be reproduced, stored in a retrieval system,
or transmitted in any form or by any means—electronic,
mechanical, photocopying, recording, or otherwise—
without the prior written permission of Lerner Publishing
Group, Inc., except for the inclusion of brief quotations in an
acknowledged review.

Twenty-First Century Books
A division of Lerner Publishing Group, Inc.
241 First Avenue North
Minneapolis, MN 55401 U.S.A.

Website address: www.lernerbooks.com

Main body text set in Bembo Std 12/15.
Typeface provided by Monotype Typography.

Library of Congress Cataloging-in-Publication Data

Gay, Kathlyn.
Food : the new gold / by Kathlyn Gay.
p.   cm.
Includes bibliographical references and index.
ISBN 978–0–7613–4607–4 (lib. bdg. : alk. paper)
1. Food security—Juvenile literature. 2. Food supply—Juvenile
literature. I. Title.
HD9000.5.G36 2013
338.1'9—dc23   2011045486

Manufactured in the United States of America
1 – DP – 7/15/12

CONTENTS

CHAPTER 1

GOING HUNGRY

Flooding in Pakistan in 2010 destroyed crops and livestock, leading to food shortages. This boy waits for a meal at a camp set up to help flood victims.

table while waiters served a sumptuous dinner consisting of nineteen different dishes. The dinner had a theme: "Blessings of the Earth and Sea." The diners were the leaders of the eight richest nations in the world—Canada, France, Germany, Italy, Japan, Russia, the United Kingdom, and the United States (the Group of Eight, or G8). They were gathered in Japan to discuss the global food crisis. According to reporters, the three-day summit cost $486 million.

Before the banquet, the leaders expressed deep concern about worldwide food shortages and rising food prices. They admonished citizens of their nations not to waste food. Then they took part in what the British newspaper the *Daily Mail* called a "gastronomic [food] extravaganza." The summit guests ate "delicacies such as caviar, milkfed lamb, sea urchin and tuna, with champagne and wines flown in from Europe and the U.S." The newspaper printed the complete menu. Critics were quick to disapprove. They "thought it hypocritical to produce such a lavish meal when world food supplies are under threat."

In contrast to the diners at the G8 summit, one billion people around the world are undernourished. Many millions more are starving, many of them babies. They lack the minimum amount of food for health and growth. Yet farmers and ranchers produce more than enough food every year to feed everyone on Earth. But much of that food does not get to the people who need it most. In some places, food has become a precious item—almost like gold.

Why do people in some parts of the world have to beg for food and sometimes even scrounge for food in garbage dumps, while people in other parts of the globe have more than enough food? They can buy almost every kind of food imaginable on grocery store shelves. Why isn't food affordable for everyone? Why

isn't it distributed to everyone equally? How can we make sure that humans have enough safe, healthy food for generations to come? How do politics, climate, and science shape food supplies? This book explores those questions and more.

DESPERATE FOR FOOD

In the Caribbean nation of Haiti, poor women cannot afford the high price of rice and other basic foods. Instead, they buy dirt; mix in vegetable shortening, salt, and water; and make cookies with it. In the Central American nations of El Salvador, Guatemala, Honduras, and Nicaragua, the cost of corn, beans, and rice has doubled in one year. People can afford only half what they could buy the year before. Eating less is their only option.

WORLD HUNGER, 2011

Less than 5% of the population is undernourished. Hunger levels are extremely low.

5–9% of the population is undernourished. Hunger levels are very low.

10–19% of the population is undernourished. Hunger levels are moderately low.

20–34% of the population is undernourished. Hunger levels are moderately high.

More than 35% of the population is undernourished. Hunger levels are very high.

Data for these nations are incomplete.

Greenland

Alaska (U.S.A.)

Canada

United States of America

Mexico

Cuba

Jamaica

Haiti

Dominican Republic

Puerto Rico

Belize

Honduras

Nicaragua

Guatemala

El Salvador

Costa Rica

Panama

Colombia

Ecuador

Peru

Venezuela

Guyana

Suriname

French Guiana

Brazil

Bolivia

Paraguay

Chile

Argentina

Uruguay

New Zealand

This Haitian woman makes mud pies for food and sets them in the sun to dry. Widespread poverty in many countries around the world means that healthy foods are unaffordable for large numbers of people.

A destitute family in Mauritania in Africa kills its goat to have meat for a few days. But by killing the goat, the family loses its supply of goat milk for breakfast. In Somalia, another African nation, people look for food in a garbage dump. Famine struck the Horn of Africa (Somalia, Ethiopia, Eritrea, and Djibouti) in 2011. More than 13 million people in this region face malnourishment and starvation. By August 2011, approximately thirty thousand children under the age of five had died from famine.

Of the seven billion people on Earth, 925 million (13 percent) suffer from hunger. Worldwide, one-third of childhood deaths result from malnutrition (unhealthy diet) and hunger-related illnesses. The main cause of hunger and starvation is poverty. Around the world, one billion people live on less than one dollar per day. Poverty itself is the result of many things, including social inequalities, government corruption, and global economics. These same forces often prevent food supplies from reaching the people who need them. And in times of warfare or natural disaster, the suffering of hungry people often worsens.

FEEDING THE WORLD'S POOR

Around the world, many organizations work to feed the hungry. On a local level, churches, food shelves, and other charitable organizations provide food within their communities. On a global level, private organizations such as Oxfam International, Bread for the World, and other groups try to alleviate widespread hunger. The United Nations (UN), an international peacekeeping and humanitarian organization, is a leading force in feeding the world's poor. For instance, the UN World Food Programme sends emergency food aid to people living with natural disasters or war.

Many governments supply food aid to poor nations. The United States provides more international food aid—about $2 billion each year—than any other country. The United States distributes this money through the U.S. Agency for International Development (USAID), which gives grants (money for specific projects) to nonprofit organizations that can transport, deliver, and distribute food in poor nations. The shipments of food generally include nonperishable (unlikely to spoil) items such as wheat, corn, peas, and lentils.

With skills learned from the International Fund for Agricultural Development (IFAD), this farmer in Sri Lanka clears an irrigation canal in his field of onions.

"TEACH A MAN TO FISH"

Have you ever heard the proverb, "Give a man a fish and you feed him for a day. Teach a man to fish and you feed him for a lifetime"? People dedicated to fighting world hunger often quote this saying. They believe that helping hungry people must involve not only giving them food but also teaching and helping them to grow or obtain their own food so they can be self-sufficient.

For example, the United Nations International Fund for Agricultural Development (IFAD) gives loans and technical assistance to poor farmers. One IFAD project loaned money to sheep farmers in a mountainous area of Tunisia in North Africa. A woman named Siham used her loan to buy four ewes (female sheep) and a ram (a male sheep). The animals mated and gave birth to more sheep. Siham sold some of the animals to be butchered for food. She sold wool from some of the other sheep to a blanket manufacturer. She used the money she earned to repay her loan and to expand her business. Over time, Siham's herd grew to sixteen sheep. With her earnings, she built a room onto her family house. She also paid for health care for her sick brother and job training for her sister. In talking about her success, she said, "I feel as if I have been reborn."

Another IFAD project brought "liquid gold"—honey—to a village in Eritrea, a country in eastern Africa. Eritrean farmers normally grow grains and beans and raise a few animals on small plots of land. But during droughts—long periods of little or no rainfall—crops won't grow and people go hungry. The IFAD project helped farmers learn to keep bees and make honey. Beekeeping enabled Hablemikael Luul, an Eritrean farmer, to survive drought. He could run his beekeeping operation with small amounts of water. Low rainfall didn't hurt his business. With the money he made selling honey, he was able to buy food—even though prices were high. "I am really happy with my new business. This is much better than working on the farm," explains Luul. "I am getting old, and farm work is really drudgery. Bee-keeping, on the other hand, requires less stamina [strength] and I make good money."

> "Good nutritious food is the very foundation of healthy children and nations. It is time for us to end hunger and malnutrition among children once and for all."
>
> —Josette Sheeran, World Food Programme executive director, 2011

Another UN agency, the UN Food and Agriculture Organization (FAO), helps farmers in poor nations around the world. FAO funds projects such as low-cost irrigation systems, which enable farmers to bring water directly to their crops during dry periods. FAO also helps farmers diversify, or vary their business operations, so they are not devastated financially if one part of their business fails. For instance, farmers might raise livestock and fish instead of just growing crops. The addition of animals to a farm not only increases business but also adds meat to a poor family's diet.

HUNGER IN THE UNITED STATES

In the United States, it is rare for people to starve to death. Still, more than thirty-five million Americans are unable to buy enough food. They often skip meals. Government officials describe these people as "food insecure," which is another way of saying they are hungry.

Food costs are rising in the United States, and the effects are obvious

A mother and daughter in the southern United States stretch the family's food assistance dollars by shopping at a discount grocery store. They will pay for the food with an electronic benefits card (below) from their state government. The card resembles a credit card.

in U.S. supermarkets. A dozen large eggs cost 93 cents in 2001. By 2011 the price was $1.84 per dozen. Milk cost $2.89 per gallon in 2001. The price had risen to $3.56 a gallon by 2011. Because of rising prices, it is common to see people using coupons for discounts on food items, buying groceries on sale, and shopping at discount food stores. Many U.S.

families—young and old, low and middle income—are trying to eat for less. The problem worsened in 2008, when the U.S. economy entered a severe recession, or downturn. Millions of people lost their jobs or saw their wages drop. Some lost their life savings. Others couldn't afford to pay for their homes.

Many of these Americans have turned for help to the Supplemental Nutrition Assistance Program (SNAP), a U.S. government food program (formerly called the Food Stamp Program). Other Americans have turned to state food assistance programs. SNAP recipients use government-issued cards (similar to credit or debit cards) to buy food.

FOOD RECYCLING

How many times have you tossed out milk, leftovers, or other food from the refrigerator because it was starting to go bad? According to a study by the USDA (U.S. Department of Agriculture), Americans throw away about 96 billion pounds (43.5 billion kilograms) of food each year. This figure includes food thrown out by U.S. supermarkets, restaurants, and households. Supermarkets throw out a lot of food because it's about to spoil and it can't be sold. Restaurants often throw away perfectly good food that customers didn't order or didn't eat. The situation is the same in other wealthy nations.

In a world where millions of people face hunger on a daily basis, the loss of so much food is a tragedy. But people are fighting the problem on many fronts. Some supermarkets send discarded fruits and vegetables to recyclers, who turn the food into nutrient-rich compost (decayed organic matter). The recyclers then send the compost to farmers, who use it as fertilizer. Some supermarkets send leftover yogurt directly to farmers, who feed it to hogs and other livestock animals.

Sometimes supermarkets must discard food that is perfectly safe to eat. For instance, food cans and boxes sometimes get damaged at stores and warehouses. Supermarkets can't sell the packages, even though the food inside them is safe. In that case, markets usually donate the food to organizations that help needy people.

Many colleges and high schools have cut cafeteria waste by serving food on dinner plates rather than on trays. Since plates hold less than trays, students are less likely to pile up food that may not be eaten. As a result, they throw away less food. Studies have shown that when students stop using trays, schools reduce food waste by 30 percent or more. Numerous universities have also built their own composting sites to turn dining hall food waste into fertilizer.

The dollar amounts vary by state and depend on the size of a family and its annual income. Because of the rising cost of food, the U.S. Congress increased SNAP funds and other essential nutrition programs in 2008. In 2011 SNAP was helping to feed more than 44 million Americans, according to the U.S. Department of Agriculture (USDA).

Other food assistance programs include federally funded school meals and the Women, Infants, and Children (WIC) program, which provides money to states to help feed pregnant women, mothers, and children. However, SNAP, WIC, and other programs are not able to provide services for all the families who are eligible. As a result, many families in the United States still do not get enough food. The USDA reports that a little more than 11 percent of U.S. households (13 million people) face food insecurity.

Students at a college in Pennsylvania empty their food waste into a bin in their dorm's dining hall. The scraps will then be used for compost.

A FOOD STAMP CHALLENGE

Since 2007 numerous federal and state officials, students, and other Americans have voluntarily participated in a program called the Food Stamp Challenge. For one week, participants are limited to spending only three dollars daily on food, the average amount a SNAP recipient receives. This effort gives participants insight into living without enough food on a daily basis.

Two *Washington Post* reporters, Kimberley Chin and Kevin McGuire, took part in the challenge. Afterward, Chin and McGuire wrote, "Living on such a budget meant meals consisting of peanut butter on white bread, night after night of pasta and drinking enormous amounts of water in an effort to fend off hunger. . . . The Food Stamp Challenge was an eye-opening experience, one that both of us were relieved to see end for ourselves. But for low-income people, making ends meet is a challenge that never ends."

U.S. representative Barbara Lee of Oakland, California, was also a participant. She reported that one day she "had grits and toast for breakfast, crackers and a banana for lunch and two hamburgers from White Castle ($.51 each) for dinner." Another day she went to a discount grocery store to buy "a small container of chicken and dumplings, an apple, a can of tuna, a box of macaroni and cheese and a can of turnip greens (total $2.25)." By the middle of the week, she reported, "It's hard to concentrate for any length of time on anything except food. I don't know how people with no money for decent meals do anything—study, work, exercise, read, have fun, etc. It's all about just making it through the day."

POVERTY, HUNGER, AND OBESITY

In the United States, obesity rates are soaring. (A person who weighs 20 percent or more above what is healthful for his or her height, age, gender, and bone structure is considered to be obese.) In 1991 four U.S. states reported that more than 15 percent of their populations were obese. By 2010 all fifty states reported obesity levels over 20 percent. Twelve states reported obesity levels over 30 percent. Approximately 17 percent of U.S. children and teens are obese.

Someone who is obese probably has plenty of food and eats too much, right? In some cases, yes. But nutrition experts and officials in charge of U.S. food aid programs point out other reasons for obesity. "Every day, I see overweight people who have empty cupboards at home," writes George A. Jones, executive director of Bread for the City, a nonprofit agency in Washington, D.C. He adds, "It's not hard to explain: the poor must eat whatever food they can access and afford; cheap, easily available food often makes for a very unhealthy diet."

Foods that a poor family can afford—such as meals from fast-food restaurants—are filling, but they are also high in calories, fat and sugar content, and low in nutrients. Nutritious, low-calorie foods, such as fresh fruits and vegetables, fish, and lean meat, cost more than fast-food "value" meals and large sodas. In addition, many inner-city neighborhoods, where poor people often live, have few supermarkets, let alone farmers' markets or natural food grocery stores. Many city dwellers don't have cars, and city public transit systems are often expensive or not very efficient. That means city dwellers cannot easily travel to quality food markets outside their neighborhoods. Think about it: how easy would it be to have to take several different city buses or subways to reach a great supermarket in a faraway neighborhood and to return home loaded down with bags of groceries? For convenience, most people will choose to shop in their own, easy-to-reach neighborhoods, even if the food choices are more expensive and not as good.

In poor neighborhoods around the United States, fast-food restaurants are common. Grocery stores and sit-down restaurants with healthier, affordable food choices are often far away and difficult to get to.

As fast-food restaurants spread around the world, obesity rates are rising there as well. The World Health Organization (WHO) estimates that around the world, 300 million people are obese—and the number is expected to more than double by 2015. As in the United States, some of this obesity is linked to malnutrition. Around the world, poor people often don't have access to healthful foods, but many, especially in big cities, have access to inexpensive fast-food restaurants. There they can load up on high-calorie, high-fat foods with poor nutritional value, just as many Americans do.

CHAPTER 2

FACTORY FARMING

*This family in the 1870s uses a McCormick reaper,
horses, and hand tools to harvest wheat on their farm.*

TWO HUNDRED YEARS AGO, most people did not have to wonder where their food came from. People around the world produced their own food supplies. Depending on where they lived, farm families raised a few pigs, ducks, cows, chickens, and other animals; grew grains to feed themselves and their animals; and tended vegetable gardens and orchards. Almost everything people ate grew on their own farm or on nearby farms. Farm families in the United States usually went to market in town on Saturday. They brought along vegetables, eggs, and a few animals to sell. The lands that people farmed usually stayed in the family. When the older generation died, the farm went to their children.

In modern times, in the United States and other rich nations, this lifestyle is long gone. In the United States, more than two million family farms still operate, but most farm families do not make much money from farming. Family members have to hold other jobs to survive. Almost no Americans are able to live off only the food they grow at home. The days when most Americans farmed and produced the majority or all of their own food supplies are over. In the twenty-first century, most of the food in the United

"The way we eat has changed more in the last 50 years than in the previous 10,000, but the image that's used to sell the food [is misleading] . . . you go into the supermarket and you see pictures of farmers [on food packaging]. The picket fence and the silo and the 1930s farmhouse and the green grass. The reality is . . . [agriculture is no longer] a farm, it's a factory. That meat is being processed by huge multi-national corporations that have very little to do with ranches and farmers."

—Michael Pollan, author, in the documentary film Food, Inc., 2008

States comes from giant agribusinesses—or farms owned by large corporations. Many of these farms are in foreign countries. How did this change happen?

CHANGING AGRICULTURAL PRACTICES

In earlier centuries, farmers used simple tools and techniques. They used horses and other strong animals to pull plows and wagons through farm fields. They planted seeds and harvested crops using simple tools. They depended on rainfall and snowfall to provide water for their crops. They used natural substances, such as animal manure, as fertilizer.

In the late 1800s and the early 1900s, farming became more mechanized and more scientific, especially in wealthy nations such as the United States. Farmers began to use chemicals to make the soil more fertile. New technology, such as motorized farm machinery, eased much of the backbreaking toil of farming and increased speed and efficiency. Mechanized irrigation systems carried more water to crops. New refrigeration techniques kept foods fresher longer in warehouses and in the trains and other vehicles that carried food to market. As a result of these changes, farmers were able to grow more food that fed more people.

Over the years, manufacturers developed better chemical fertilizers. They also developed chemical pesticides (bug killers) and herbicides (weed killers). These products improved crop yields even more. Agriculture specialists crossbred different varieties of seeds to produce stronger and more nutritious food plants. Farmers fattened their livestock with new and improved feed developed by agricultural firms. They fended off animal diseases with a variety of drugs.

Farmers also took advantage of economies of scale. They learned that raising crops and livestock in large quantities reduces the per-unit cost of producing each item. For instance, it costs less per cow to raise fifty cows at once than to raise one cow at a time. So farmers began to operate more like manufacturers. They learned to control as much of the production process as possible.

In the mid-twentieth century, big companies bought up many small family farms. The companies created giant agribusinesses, with fields spread over vast areas. Some agribusinesses branched out from farming into food processing, marketing, and distribution.

FEWER FISHERIES

One in five people on Earth depend on fish as a primary source of protein. More than 150 million people make their living by fishing. But overfishing has depleted the world's fisheries—oceans, rivers, and other natural bodies of water where fish are normally caught. According to the FAO, more than 25 percent of the world's fisheries are overexploited. That is, the fish there are being taken from the water faster than new fish are being born. In addition, water pollution has damaged many fisheries. Global climate change has also warmed many bodies of water, making them uninhabitable for certain species of fish.

In the fisheries of the North Atlantic Ocean, populations of commercial cod, haddock, and flounder have fallen by as much as 95 percent. This situation has spelled economic disaster for people who normally make their living by fishing. Consumers have also suffered because with fewer fish in the world's lakes and oceans, the price of fish has risen steeply.

With the decrease in natural fisheries, many people have turned to aquaculture, or fish farming, to raise fish and other seafood. Aquaculturists grow fish in artificial ponds or sometimes in nets or cages in natural bodies of water. In the first decade of the twenty-first century, about one-fourth of the seafood eaten on Earth came from fish farms.

The growth of big fish farms has further hurt traditional fishing businesses. Not only have their natural fisheries been depleted, but small, traditional fishers can't compete with large fish farms, which use economies of scale to minimize their production costs and their prices.

This man feeds fish at a fish farm off the coast of Mauritius, an island nation in the Indian Ocean. Aquaculture is a growing industry. In just one year, this farm doubled the number of fish it produced.

These changes were most pronounced in the United States and other big wealthy nations. Big U.S. companies sometimes bought vast tracts of land in poor nations and began to operate agribusinesses there as well.

AGRIBUSINESS

In the United States and other wealthy nations, the modern farm is a far cry from the family farm of the 1800s. Many modern farms are owned by international corporations. Most farms specialize in growing one type of crop, such as corn, soybeans, or wheat. Large-scale "field factories" grow lettuce, tomatoes, strawberries, and other vegetables and fruits on a massive scale. Giant "factory farms" or "animal factories" breed, raise, slaughter, and process cattle, pigs, poultry, and other animals for food using assembly-line techniques. Many big farms grow food to supply just one large corporation. For instance, Lopez Foods of Oklahoma City, Oklahoma, raises cattle just to supply hamburger meat to McDonald's. The fast-food chain's chicken comes from Pennsylvania-based Keystone Foods; its potatoes come from Saddle View Farms of Warden, Washington; and its lettuce comes from Christensen & Giannini of Salinas, California.

Most modern agribusinesses do much more than farm. Many own or invest in seed and animal feed companies, grain mills, breeding operations, slaughterhouses, food-processing plants, and agricultural research. The corporate executives who run large-scale modern farms often live and work far away from the operations they control. They have little if any contact with people in the rural towns affected by the huge operations. Unlike farmers in previous centuries, they do not handle the hard, day-to-day work of planting and picking crops, milking cows, or slaughtering animals.

Big corporate farming began to dominate agriculture in the 1960s and the 1970s. Using economies of scale, large farms could produce crops and livestock quickly, in large numbers, and inexpensively. Owners of small farms could not compete with the large firms. Many went out of business. Others sold their operations to the big companies and stayed on as employees. For example, huge poultry operations opened in rural areas across the southeastern United States in the 1980s and the 1990s. Alabama, Arkansas, Mississippi, Georgia, Delaware, Maryland, Virginia, West Virginia, and Texas saw a rapid expansion of poultry production.

CITY CHICKENS

In the United States of the 1800s, chickens, cows, hogs, and other livestock were not confined on corporate farms as they are in the twenty-first century. City dwellers often kept livestock at their homes. The animals even meandered through streets and parks in New York City. As U.S. cities got more crowded in the early 1900s, lawmakers passed rules against urban livestock.

But in modern times, a new trend is emerging, and farm animals are reappearing in some cities. In the second decade of the twenty-first century, seventeen U.S. cities, including Key West, Florida; Seattle, Washington; San Francisco, California; Chicago, Illinois; Minneapolis, Minnesota; and New York, New York, allow residents to raise chickens in their yards. The chickens provide people with free fresh eggs—straight from the bird rather than trucked in from a far-off farm and then purchased in a food store. And chicken owners can give the birds a healthy, chemical-free, drug-free diet, ensuring that the eggs will also be free of drugs and chemicals.

A mother and daughter feed their chickens in the backyard of their Florida home. Many U.S. cities allow families to keep chickens.

Tyson Foods, with headquarters in Arkansas, is the world's largest processor of poultry and other meats. Tyson processes more than 41 million chickens each week. Like most other chicken producers, Tyson pays farmers in various states to produce its chickens and eggs. The farms include huge buildings to house thousands of hens and roosters. Chickens receive nourishment through automatic feeding and watering lines. The birds live most of their lives inside the buildings. Tyson provides feed, medicine, and other supplies to care for the chickens. After the birds are grown, they are transported from farms to processing plants, where they are slaughtered and turned into chicken nuggets, chicken patties, and other products.

CAFOS

Agribusiness began running massive indoor livestock operations, with tens of thousands of animals, in the 1970s. As these concentrated animal feeding operations (CAFOs) opened, more family-owned farms went out of business. They could not afford to compete with corporate meat producers.

Pigs in concentrated animal feeding operations (CAFOs) live their entire short lives in indoor metal and concrete pens. They are typically slaughtered when they are six months old.

For a better understanding of CAFOs, take a look at a typical U.S. hog factory. It is usually part of a major meat-processing company. The company supervises construction of metal buildings to house the hogs. Lined up one after the other in rows, the buildings look like barracks or warehouses. Some buildings are as big as football fields. Each can hold eight hundred to one thousand hogs.

Inside the buildings, hogs live in elevated steel pens. Grates underneath their feet allow feces and urine to fall through to a concrete floor below. Several times each day, workers flush this waste from the buildings. Pipes carry the waste to nearby ponds, called lagoons. The buildings have separate rooms for boars (male hogs) and for sows (female hogs).

The buildings are usually well lit and clean. Staff members control the indoor temperature, humidity, and other environmental factors and monitor hogs for possible health threats. In many operations, visitors must wear sterile coveralls over their street clothes to avoid contaminating the hogs with disease-causing viruses or bacteria. The operators' main concern is keeping the animals healthy so they bring the best possible price when sold and sent to slaughterhouses. A hog is ready for market when it weighs about 250 pounds (113 kg).

With their huge operations, CAFOs are able to raise many animals at low cost and to sell pork and other meat at low prices. This business model is spreading around the world. Since the 1990s, major corporations have opened CAFOs in Asia, eastern Europe, and Latin America to meet a growing worldwide demand for beef, pork, and poultry. In 1990 Asia produced 24.4 percent of the world's poultry. By 2007 that number had jumped to 35.5 percent. In Latin America, the figure rose from 10.9 percent to 17 percent in that same time span. Between 2008 and 2018, chicken production is expected to grow by more than 20 percent in Brazil, by more than 28.4 percent in China, and by more than 30 percent in India.

> "Only 'industrial farming' can possibly meet the demands of an increasing population and increased demand for food."
>
> —Blake Hurst, Missouri farmer, 2009

CHAPTER 3

INDUSTRIAL FARMING:
HAZARDOUS TO YOUR HEALTH?

Veal calves are often locked in small wooden crates or pens. They do not have room to move around.

activists have decried the treatment of animals in factory farms. Observers have reported pregnant animals locked in narrow cages, animals standing in their own urine and feces, and farmworkers cruelly mistreating animals. In late November 2011, the animal rights group Mercy for Animals released undercover footage taken at Sparboe Farms facilities in Minnesota, Iowa, and Colorado. Sparboe supplied eggs to McDonald's, Target, and a number of grocery store chains. First aired on the TV show *20/20*, the footage showed hens crammed into tiny metal cages, feces- and blood-coated eggs, and carcasses of long-dead hens under the feet of live egg-producing chickens.

The exposé led to some changes. McDonald's and other major customers stopped doing business with Sparboe. But animal rights activists note that similar mistreatment still occurs at other factory farms.

WORST OF THE WORST?

Many activists say that veal farms, where calves (baby cows) are raised for meat, are among the most extreme examples of animal cruelty on factory farms. Animal rights activists call veal production "one of the most bizarre agricultural practices ever developed." They note that calves live in misery for about sixteen weeks (from birth until slaughter), until they reach about 350 to 400 pounds (159 to 181 kg).

Veal is prized for its light-colored meat. So veal calves are never allowed outside, where they might eat grass, which will darken their flesh. Instead, calves live indoors in steel stalls without their mothers. The stalls have no straw bedding, because if calves ate the straw, that too would discolor their meat. The stalls are so small that calves are forced to stand up. Many calves end up crippled from confinement and lack of proper nutrition.

Veal is more popular in Europe than in the United States, and European veal producers there have recently instituted more humane practices. In 2007 veal producers in the European Union (EU, an association of European nations) phased out individual crates for calves in favor of more spacious housing, with room for four to seven animals. In the United Kingdom, calves are given straw bedding, despite the risk of darkening their meat. In France some producers allow calves to stay with their mothers and drink mothers' milk.

In the United States, practices have been slow to change, however. Only a few states have outlawed veal crates. And the American Veal Association (AVA) defends its members' practices. An AVA pamphlet declares that steel stalls are necessary to keep veal calves safe and healthy:

> [AVA] guidelines support the practice of raising calves in individual stalls because it allows farmers to carefully monitor and control the calf's nutritional and health status. Calves have a very strong sucking instinct and contact between calves . . . greatly increases their likelihood of contracting disease. In fact, studies show that calves raised in groups have from two to 14 times the disease rate of individually penned calves. For this and other reasons—including ease of cleaning and feeding—veal calves are housed individually in their own pens. . . . Each stall is constructed so that the calves will have adequate room to stand, stretch, step forward, backward, and from side to side, lie in a natural position and groom themselves. Slotted flooring is provided for comfort and cleanliness.

WORKERS AT RISK

"Slaughtering swine is repetitive, brutish work, so grueling that three weeks on the factory floor leave no doubt in your mind about why the turnover [of workers] is 100 percent. Five thousand quit and five thousand are hired every year." Those words come from *New York Times* investigative journalist Charlie LeDuff, reporting on working conditions in large-scale industrialized food production. In industries such as meatpacking, workers labor in bloody, greasy, damp, and cold facilities. LeDuff described Smithfield Foods' hog slaughtering house, the largest in the world, near Chapel Hill, North Carolina:

You hear people say, they don't kill pigs in the plant, they kill people. . . .
The work burns your muscles and dulls your mind. Staring down into
the meat for hours strains your neck. After thousands of cuts a day your
fingers no longer open freely. Standing in the damp [cold] air causes your
knees to lock, your nose to run, your teeth to throb.

Chicken handlers, whose job is to gather chickens and put them in cages before slaughtering, are also subject to health and safety hazards. They handle as many as thirty to fifty thousand live chickens per shift. The work exposes them to dust, flying feathers, pecking from the birds, and choking ammonia from chicken manure. Many workers develop respiratory diseases and other illnesses from exposure to chicken manure and harmful bacteria.

Workers at slaughterhouses, chicken farms, and other agricultural businesses do not stay long at the job because it is so difficult. As a result, the companies need to regularly find new workers. Replacements are not hard to find. Many workers in U.S. agribusiness are immigrants from Mexico or from nations in Southeast Asia, Central America, or Africa. U.S. companies recruit immigrants because they often will work for low

The labor at a meatpacking plant is physically demanding. In this Colorado plant, workers cut huge sides of beef into smaller steaks and roasts. They use sharp knives and work in cold temperatures. Health hazards of the job include cuts, falls, and stiff joints.

pay and few benefits. Even dangerous, low-paying meatpacking jobs are often better than jobs available in the immigrants' countries of origin. "New arrivals may have low expectations and be willing to endure conditions . . . that American workers would not willingly tolerate," reports the U.S. Congressional Research Service.

In addition, some of the immigrants are in the United States illegally and rely on falsified employment documents to get jobs. They are afraid to complain about unsafe working conditions for fear that U.S. officials will discover their illegal status and send them back to their home countries. They are right to worry. In several well-publicized cases, U.S. Immigrations and Customs Enforcement (ICE) agents raided meatpacking companies and arrested illegal workers. In 2006 ICE arrested almost thirteen hundred employees of Swift & Company at its facilities in Colorado, Iowa, Texas, Minnesota, and Nebraska. More than half of those arrested were deported (sent back to their home countries). In 2008 ICE raided Agriprocessors Inc., a slaughterhouse in Postville, Iowa. It arrested 389 people. Nearly all of them were deported.

FAST WORK

The faster a meat or poultry facility can process animals, the more money it will make. Carcasses move quickly along conveyor belts. Workers must cut and trim the meat at lightning speed. At some plants, supervisors scream at line workers to move faster and faster. A worker in a beef processing plant repeated her supervisor's demands: "'Speed, Ruth, work for speed!' he shouted as he stood over me. 'One cut! One cut! One cut for the skin; one cut for the meat. Get those pieces through!'"

Such conditions lead to frequent injuries. Workers in meat processing plants stand close to one another, often accidentally cutting one another with sharp knives and saws. The repetitive motions required of meatcutters can cause injuries such as tendonitis and carpal tunnel syndrome— numbness, tingling, and pain in the wrist and hand, sometimes radiating up the arm. Floors are often slippery with blood and grease, which leads to falls and other accidents, sometimes causing serious injuries.

According to some analysts, the U.S. meat and poultry industries keep labor costs low by offering workers little or no health-care benefits and doing little or nothing to provide safe working conditions. *Blood, Sweat and Fear,* a report by the international agency Human Rights Watch, describes the "thousands of lacerations [cuts], contusions [bruises], burns, fractures [broken bones], punctures and other forms of what the medical profession calls traumatic injuries" endured by meat and poultry workers. Yet most workers are afraid to complain because they fear they will lose their jobs.

CAFO CONTAMINATION

One of the most troubling aspects of factory farming is animal waste from CAFOs. A large CAFO can generate from 2,800 to 1.6 million tons (2,540 to 1.45 million metric tons) of manure a year, more than the yearly human waste produced by some U.S. cities. CAFO operators collect animal waste in lagoons, some of which cover up to 1 acre (0.4 hectares) of land. Animal waste contains chemicals such as phosphorus and nitrogen, which can be good fertilizers. So CAFOs send the waste from manure lagoons to fertilize nearby farmland.

But manure and wastewater from CAFOs can also contain harmful substances, such as pathogens (bacteria or viruses that cause disease), heavy metals, hormones, and ammonia. On several occasions, CAFO waste used to fertilize vegetable farms has contaminated the vegetables with deadly strains of *Escherichia coli* (*E. coli*) bacteria.

Sometimes waste from CAFOs runs off farmland into streams and rivers. It can also seep into aquifers—underground sources of drinking

Waste from a dairy farm in Maryland sits in a treatment pond. Workers will pump out the waste to use as fertilizer in farm fields.

water. Many huge U.S. CAFO operations are located in the Delmarva Peninsula, which includes Delaware, eastern Maryland, and part of Virginia. This region frequently floods. When it does, waste from CAFOs sometimes pollutes waterways and soils.

Plants and animals need nitrogen and phosphorus for growth, but CAFO waste often contains excessive nitrogen and phosphorus. When this waste ends up in water, the results can be harmful. Too much nitrogen or phosphorus can cause algae and other aquatic plants to grow rapidly. These plants decay quickly and, in the process, use up the water's oxygen supply. As a result, fish and other aquatic life don't get enough oxygen and die.

In addition to animal waste, gases and dust from CAFOs can pose health hazards. Dust from cattle feedlots (where animals are fattened for market) and from poultry and hog industries often contains bacteria, mold, and fungi, which can make people sick. At huge cattle feedlots, such as those in hot and dry western Texas, thousands of tons of manure dust fill the air. The dust (and smell of manure) rises and travels with the wind for miles, sometimes sickening people who live downwind.

Between 1982 and 2002, the number of CAFOs in the United States increased from about thirty-six hundred to almost twelve thousand, according to the U.S. Government Accountability Office (GAO). By 2011 more than fifteen thousand CAFOs were operating in the United States. As CAFOs have grown larger and more numerous, the environmental risks have risen as well. The GAO reports that since 2002, at least sixty-eight studies have "examined air and water quality issues associated with animal feeding operations and 15 have directly linked air and water pollutants from animal waste to specific health or environmental impacts."

"When we overcrowd thousands of animals into cramped filthy football-field sized sheds to lie beak-to-beak, or snout-to-snout atop their own waste it can present a breeding ground for disease, a perfect storm environment for the emergence of new strains of influenza and other animal-to-human diseases. These so-called factory farms are a public health menace."

—*Michael Greger, physician, 2011*

GOING GLOBAL

As CAFOs have expanded around the world, the hazards—to both workers and the environment—have gone global as well. In developing CAFOs, multinational corporations search worldwide to find large land areas for raising livestock. They also look for a large supply of workers to hire for low wages. Finally, they look for areas where environmental, worker safety, and animal welfare laws are lax so they don't have to comply with strict government regulations. The corporations find these conditions in poor nations in Latin America and in eastern Europe. Many poor nations are eager to have the jobs offered by CAFOs, no matter how bad the repercussions. The Pew Research Center explains the situation:

> In the developing world [poor nations], governments and workers often do not have the ability or resources to enforce environmental, worker safety, or animal welfare laws, if they even exist. Or if a country does have the capacity, it often chooses not to enforce regulations in the belief that the economic benefits of a CAFO offset any detrimental [harmful] impacts. But unregulated CAFO facilities can have disastrous consequences for the people living and working around them. Rivers used for washing and drinking may be polluted. Workers may be exposed to diseases and other hazards that they neither recognize nor understand because of their limited education.

In addition to causing pollution and endangering workers, overseas CAFOs have hurt small farms, just as they have done in the United States. In the late 1990s and the early 2000s, U.S. CAFOs operator Smithfield opened hog farms in the eastern European nations of Poland and Romania. In Romania small hog farms were unable to compete with the CAFOs. The numbers of Romanian hog farms fell from almost five hundred thousand to about fifty thousand in just a few years. Similar statistics come from Poland. The eastern European CAFOs have also exported low-priced frozen pork to African nations. Once again, local pork producers there can't compete with the low prices, and many have gone out of business.

The Philippines, an island nation in eastern Asia, has seen the establishment of many CAFOs in the 2000s. Some CAFOs have brought in foreign breeds of poultry and other livestock to raise in

U.S.-based corporate farming is expanding all over the world. For example, this new CAFO operation is in Poland.

their operations. Some of these animals carry diseases that were previously unknown in the Philippines. These diseases have sickened and killed some local livestock, which has no immunity (resistance) to them. In addition, the CAFOs have put many small-scale Philippine farmers out of business. As in the United States, the CAFOs produce large amounts of animal waste, which pollutes local land and water. Despite these hazards, the Philippine people are reluctant to complain about CAFOs, since they bring jobs and other economic benefits to communities.

TROUBLE IN THE FIELDS

Hazards also exist for workers in field factories. Most of those who plant and pick fruits and vegetables at large U.S. farms are immigrants from Mexico or from nations in South America. The workers travel from one region of the United States to another, following planting and harvesting cycles.

These migrant (traveling) farmworkers are among the lowest paid in the U.S. labor force. They often work ten to twelve hours a day. Farm operators do not provide them with health insurance or other benefits. Most farmworkers are not represented by labor unions (workers' rights organizations).

THE GREEN REVOLUTION— PROS AND CONS

After World War II (1939–1945), U.S. scientists launched a "Green Revolution" to fight food shortages in Asia and Latin America. Researchers developed new varieties of wheat and rice that produced much more grain than previous varieties. When farmers in poor nations began using these grains, their food yields soared. The larger harvests saved millions from starvation.

But the new grains had disadvantages. Unlike native-grown grains, they did not reseed themselves (grow without new seed being planted) year after year. Farmers had to buy new seeds each year. In addition, the new crop varieties required more fertilizer and more water than the old, native crops did. The new varieties also needed large quantities of pesticides to resist local insects and other pests. They required more herbicides because weed growth increases with the heavy use of fertilizers.

Since the Green Revolution, farmers in poor countries have become more and more dependent on international agribusinesses for their agricultural supplies. They need large amounts of fertilizers, pesticides, and herbicides to grow modern varieties of grain. They also need large irrigation systems

Agronomist (food scientist) Norman Borlaug is pictured in 1970 inspecting grains he developed. Borlaug is called the father of the Green Revolution. He won a Nobel Prize for his work in 1970.

to supply extra water. Most farmers in poor countries cannot afford these products and systems. And as in the United States, the largest overseas farms—often owned by international corporations—have been able to prosper using economies of scale, while many small family farms have failed.

Migrant workers pick strawberries (top) in California. The fields are usually sprayed heavily (below) with toxic pesticides to prevent insects and other pests from destroying the crops.

Migrant farmworkers face many health and safety hazards on the job. Field factories often lack adequate toilets, drinking water, and hand-washing facilities for workers. When farm laborers do not have sufficient drinking water, they can become dehydrated or suffer other heat-related health problems. Working with unclean hands, farm laborers can spread diseases to one another and to the food they handle.

Most big U.S. farms spray chemical pesticides and herbicides to protect crops from insects and weeds. But in high concentrations, these chemicals can be toxic, or poisonous, to people. Chemical pesticides and herbicides have seeped into waterways, polluting them and poisoning drinking water.

Federal regulations require that farmworkers stay out of fields for a specific length of time after pesticide spraying, but many farm operators don't follow the rules and don't warn workers about the dangers. Each year, tens of thousands of farmworkers suffer illnesses due to pesticide exposure. No one knows the exact number of poisonings because victims seldom seek medical care. They rarely have health insurance and are reluctant to miss work to visit a doctor. And even when farmworkers do seek medical care, doctors may fail to diagnose pesticide poisoning accurately because symptoms are similar to those associated with the flu.

Outside the United States, field workers face the same dangers from pesticides—but sometimes on a much larger scale. In the late twentieth century, the South and Central American banana industry was notorious for exposing workers to pesticides. At its banana plantations in Nicaragua, the U.S.-based Dole Food Company used a toxic pesticide that had been banned in the United States. A number of workers eventually took Dole to court, charging that exposure to toxic chemicals had made them sterile (unable to have children), had given them cancer, or had caused birth defects in their babies. Although some of the cases were dismissed, other workers won large cash settlements from the company.

In the twenty-first century, the situation for Latin American banana workers is only slightly improved. Banana growers still use a variety of herbicides, pesticides, and fungicides (to kill fungus) on their banana trees. For protection from toxins, workers are supposed to wear full-body coveralls, rubber gloves, boots, and respirators. But many growers don't provide this gear to their workers.

CONSUMER BEWARE

Many critics charge that food from factory farms can also harm the consumer—the person who eats the food. For example, scientists are concerned about the increasing use of antibiotics (drugs that kill certain bacteria) in meat animals.

For decades, producers of farm animals have used antibiotics to treat infections, especially in chickens and hogs. Producers also use antibiotics on healthy hogs, cattle, veal calves, and poultry to prevent illness and because the drugs help quickly fatten the animals. But experts say that high levels of antibiotics in farm animals may lead to serious health risks for people. Antibiotics remain in animal wastes that run off into waterways and underground water sources. In addition, overuse of antibiotics can make them ineffective. The drugs no longer kill off the bacteria they're intended to kill—and some of these drug-resistant bacteria can sicken both people and animals. Thus when food producers overuse antibiotics with animals, they also put people at risk.

A 2011 study published in the journal *Clinical Infectious Diseases* examined samples of meat and poultry for sale in twenty-six U.S. grocery stores. The study found antibiotic-resistant bacteria in about one-quarter of the food. Although the bacteria would normally be killed off with proper cooking, the statistic alarmed both public health experts and consumers.

Bacteria aren't the only hazards passed on to consumers through CAFO-raised livestock. CAFOs feed grain to their livestock, and these grains are usually treated with a lot of pesticides and fertilizers in the fields where they grow. When animals eat the grains, the chemicals from the pesticides and fertilizers accumulate in their body fat. When humans in turn eat the animals, they also consume the chemicals. Studies have linked such chemicals to cancer and other diseases. You are what you eat eats, stresses author Michael Pollan in his book *In Defense of Food: An Eater's Manifesto.* Pollan encourages consumers to shun CAFO-raised livestock and factory-farmed grain to keep agricultural chemicals from accumulating in their bodies.

"American dairy farms are one of the most regulated and inspected industries in agriculture. . . . Most dairy producers—regardless of farm size—live and work to protect the land, water, and air. . . . Barns are built and managed with animal comfort and care as the first priority. . . . We provide the cattle with mattresses to lounge on, bed the stalls with fresh sawdust, and ventilate the facility so that there are constant air exchanges. . . . The calves and cows are not restrained and always have access to ample feed and fresh water."

—*Meg Gaige, dairy farmer and agricultural reporter, defending dairy CAFOs, 2008*

Some large dairies inject cows with a substance called recombinant bovine growth hormone (rBGH), which increases the cows' milk production. The multinational Missouri-based Monsanto Corporation developed rBGH and markets it under the brand name Posilac. In 1993 the Food and Drug Administration (FDA), an agency that oversees the safety of food and medicine in the United States, approved the use of rBGH, stating that it was not harmful to cows or to humans that drank milk from cows treated with the hormone.

But numerous animal welfare, consumer, environmental, and medical groups strongly disagree with the FDA. They say that rBGH poses cancer risks to humans. In addition, they argue that rBGH interferes with a cow's natural physiology. That is, the hormone makes the cow produce more milk than is natural for her body, making the animal more susceptible to infection and disease. To treat cows that get sick, dairy farmers must use more antibiotics, possibly leading to drug-resistant bacteria that can threaten human health.

Many people don't want to drink milk with rBGH, and since the 1990s, dairies that don't use the hormone have stated so on their milk cartons. Monsanto has lobbied to forbid the use of such labels, because they imply that rBGH is unsafe. A number of states have tried to ban the rBGH labeling, but consumer groups and others have thwarted the efforts.

Because of consumer pressure, U.S. supermarkets such as Safeway, Walmart, and Kroger no longer sell dairy products made with rBGH, and in 2008 Monsanto itself gave up the fight for the hormone. The corporation sold its rBGH operations to Elanco, which is part of Indianapolis-based Eli Lilly and Company. Elanco continues to sell milk with rBGH, insisting that it poses no risks to human or animal health.

Milk cartons include labeling to let consumers know if the milk was made from cows treated with rBGH growth hormone.

CHAPTER 4

CLIMATE CRISIS

Frequent and severe droughts are among the crises that scientists have predicted as an outcome of global warming. This Kenyan farmer walks through a field of parched maize (corn) during a severe drought in eastern Africa. The drought left millions of people in need of food aid.

warning that climate change—the warming of Earth's atmosphere—would lead to droughts and other weather catastrophes. By 2010 those predictions appeared to be coming true. A severe drought struck Russia—a vast nation straddling Europe and western Asia—in 2010. Wildfires consumed fields of crops, while other crops shriveled up in the dry soil and intense heat. The following year, 2011, the U.S. state of Texas was hit hard by drought. From January to November, Texas received just 46 percent of its normal rainfall.

The situation was much worse in northeastern Africa. In 2011 it experienced its worst drought in sixty years. The lack of rainfall prevented people in Ethiopia, Somalia, Kenya, and Djibouti from harvesting a sufficient supply of crops and from raising healthy livestock. Food shortages led to rapidly rising prices for grains such as sorghum and maize. At one point, grain prices in Somalia increased by 240 percent. In Ethiopia the increase was 117 percent, and in Kenya, it was 58 percent. With shortages and soaring food prices, people began to starve.

Many people say that climate change is the cause of all this suffering—and that we've seen only just the beginning of it. What's causing the climate to change? The answer lies in the greenhouse effect.

THE GREENHOUSE EFFECT AND GLOBAL WARMING

Scientists link climate change to the atmosphere, the layer of gases surrounding Earth. These gases include oxygen, nitrogen, hydrogen, carbon dioxide, water vapor, methane, and ozone. Sunlight passes through the gases to warm Earth. Some of the gases in the atmosphere also trap heat near Earth, keeping it from escaping back into space.

A similar process happens in a greenhouse. The sun's light and heat pass through the glass roof of the greenhouse. But the same glass keeps the heat from escaping, so the inside of the greenhouse stays warm. In 1896 Swedish chemist Svante Arrhenius was the first person to note the similarity between Earth's atmosphere and a greenhouse. He coined the term *greenhouse effect*. The gases that trap heat near Earth are called greenhouse gases.

The greenhouse effect on Earth is a natural condition. Without greenhouse gases, too much heat would escape from Earth back into space. Earth would probably be too cold to sustain life.

For millions of years, the atmosphere has basically had the same amount of greenhouse gases as an overall percentage of the atmosphere. But starting in the late 1700s, rich nations such as the United States became industrialized. People began to burn more fossil fuels—coal, oil, and natural gas—to run furnaces, vehicles, and other machines. Burning fossil fuels releases carbon dioxide into the atmosphere. Over several hundred years, the extra carbon dioxide has intensified the greenhouse effect. The atmosphere has started trapping more heat, creating higher temperatures on Earth. Scientists call this process global warming.

Scientists first identified global warming in the late 1970s. In 1988 the United Nations formed the Intergovernmental Panel on Climate Change (IPCC), which includes more than twenty-five hundred scientists and technicians from varied fields, such as climatology, ecology, economics, medicine, and oceanography. In 2001 the panel said that if no actions were taken to reduce global warming, average global temperatures could rise between 1.4 and 5.8°C (2.5 to 10°F) by the end of the twenty-first century.

Scientists also said that global warming could lead to more extreme weather, such as hurricanes, floods, droughts, and severe storms. They also predicted that rising temperatures would cause ice to melt at the North Pole and the South Pole. The melting ice would flood into oceans, causing sea levels to rise.

These predictions seem to be coming true. In 2007 the IPCC stated: "Warming of the climate system is unequivocal [certain], as is now evident from observations of increases in global average air and ocean temperatures, widespread melting of snow and ice and rising global average sea level."

THE IMPACT OF HUMAN ACTIVITIES ON THE GREENHOUSE EFFECT

Less heat energy escapes into space due to the "dirtying" of the infrared "window."

Incoming solar energy

Burning of fossil fuels, industry, agriculture, and deforestation increase the amounts of CO_2 and other greenhouse gases in the atmosphere. Increased amounts of greenhouse gases absorb more of the heat energy radiated by Earth's surface.

Infrared (heat) energy is radiated by the warmed Earth surface.

More heat is reradiated back toward Earth, causing air and surface temperatures to rise.

WATER:
TOO LITTLE AND TOO MUCH

Scientists say that higher temperatures on Earth will bring heat waves to many areas. And the extra heat will dry up existing water sources, leading to droughts and water shortages. "As the planet warms, look for . . . deeper drought where water is scarce," writes Elizabeth Kolbert in *National Geographic*.

"Two-thirds of the world's population will face a lack of water in less than 20 years, if current trends in climate change . . . continue," warns UN deputy secretary-general Asha-Rose Migiro. She stresses that "1.8 billion people will be living in countries or regions with water scarcity by 2025."[22] Because of expected shortages, people sometimes call freshwater blue gold or the new oil—just as precious as gold or the fuel we need to run our cars.

Water shortages are already a reality in the western United States. In California, Arizona, Colorado, Nevada, New Mexico, Utah, and Wyoming, water supplies come from snow falling in the Rocky Mountains and the Sierra Nevada. The snow melts in spring and runs into rivers. But higher temperatures in the early 2000s have reduced runoff in western mountains. Instead of melting, mountain snow has evaporated—or turned into water vapor. As a result, less snow melts and runs into rivers that supply western populations with water.

In polar regions, giant ice sheets are melting, leading to rising sea levels. Here, meltwater pours off a glacier, a slow-moving body of ice.

While some areas of the world are experiencing water shortages due to global warming, other regions could soon be under water. With the rise in global temperatures, ice around the North Pole and the South Pole has begun to melt, with the water running off into oceans and causing sea levels to rise.

No one is certain how much sea levels could rise. The IPCC estimates that by the end of the twenty-first century, sea levels could rise from 7 to 23 inches (18 to 59 centimeters). In one scenario described by the U.S. Environmental Protection Agency, EPA, the rise could be as high as 40 inches (101 cm). A 2009 report in *Science* says that if the West Antarctic Ice Sheet melted, sea levels would rise 11 feet (3.4 meters). If that scenario were to come true, major U.S. cities such as New York, New York; Los Angeles, California, and Miami, Florida, could end up under water. That same thing would happen to other coastal cities, including Calcutta, India; Shanghai, China; Tokyo, Japan; and Jakarta, Indonesia.

The U.S. National Aeronautics and Space Administration (NASA) says that polar ice has been melting more quickly than expected. David Hik of the International Polar Year project told a British reporter, "What

"The warnings about global warming have been extremely clear for a long time. We are facing a global climate crisis. It is deepening. We are entering a period of consequences."

—Al Gore, former U.S. vice president and subject of An Inconvenient Truth
(a 2006 Academy Award–winning documentary film about global warming), 2005

happens at the poles will influence all parts of the planet and it's very evident that we can see rapid changes in sea level associated with changes in the Arctic and Antarctic."

EFFECTS ON AGRICULTURE

What about the effects of global warming on agriculture? Some scientists say that a warmer climate could benefit farms in some parts of the world. For instance, in the U.S. Great Lakes region and in eastern Canada, warmer temperatures would mean a longer growing season. Farmers could produce more grains and other crops.

But in other areas, such as California, climate change has already started to hurt agriculture. California is the largest producer of vegetable and fruit crops in the United States. But since 2007, water shortages in California have crippled the state's agricultural production. Because of drought, farmers haven't been able to plant hundreds of thousands of acres in the state's Central Valley. As farmers have struggled to survive, field workers, food processors, and food packers have also lost jobs. Businesses in farming towns have closed. Some communities have enacted water restrictions, limiting amounts that homes and businesses can use. California lost hundreds of millions of dollars due to drought in 2008 and 2009. The effects of the drought were still being felt in 2011. Many California communities still had water restrictions in place, and high prices for fruit and vegetables were still evident in supermarkets.

When drought hit Russia in 2011, millions of acres of grain crops were lost. Grain prices soared. Farmers didn't have enough barley to feed to their livestock, so consumers faced shortages of meat and poultry in supermarkets. The same year in Texas, farmers lost an estimated $5.2 billion due to the dry conditions. Ranchers across the state were forced to sell or slaughter six hundred thousand cows because they didn't have enough food and water to keep the animals healthy enough to bring to market.

CROPS FOR FOOD
OR FUEL?

Biofuels, or fuels made from plants and plant products, offer advantages over fossil fuels such as coal, oil, and natural gas. While supplies of Earth's fossil fuels are limited, biofuels are renewable. That is, when biofuels run out, people can grow more plants to replace them.

Ethanol is a common biofuel. It is produced from corn and sugarcane. Biodiesel, another kind of biofuel, is made from vegetable oils. Nonedible plant materials, including leaves, tree bark, sawdust, wood chips, and even algae, can also be turned into biofuel. Even rotting garbage from landfills can be turned into biofuel.

Around the world, biofuel production and use is increasing. The United States and Brazil account for 87 percent of the world's ethanol production. European nations account for 65 percent of biodiesel production. The Chinese airline Air China has started using algae-based biofuels to fuel airplanes. In the United States, United Airlines and Alaska Airlines also offer biofuel-powered flights. Many automobiles can run on ethanol fuel, but in the United States, most fuel for cars contains only a small amount of ethanol.

As the demand for biofuels has grown, many farmers have given up producing food crops and have started growing corn, sugarcane, and other crops that can be turned into fuel. For many years, the United States gave tax breaks and other financial incentives to ethanol producers, partly to reduce U.S. dependence on foreign oil. The practice was controversial, however. Critics said the government shouldn't encourage farmers to grow crops for fuel when millions of people worldwide drastically need food. Partly in response to this criticism, in 2011 the United States stopped its incentives for ethanol producers.

Record heat waves hit central and southern parts of the United States in 2011. The heat led to drought, which led to shortages of vital water, hay, and grass for livestock such as these cattle in Texas.

The drought also hit Kansas that year. Because water and hay were in short supply, Kansas ranchers couldn't afford to take care of their cattle either. They too sold and slaughtered cattle in record numbers that year.

EFFECTS OF FLOODING

While some places suffer from drought, global warming is also expected to bring floods and rising sea levels to other areas. Rising sea levels could flood coastal farmlands, fisheries, and wetlands. Wetlands are breeding areas for fish, shrimps, crabs, ducks, geese, and other animals that people use as food. Saltwater intrusion—the movement of ocean water into freshwater coastal wetlands—would destroy these wetlands and the plants and animals that make their homes there, because these living things won't be able to tolerate the salty ocean water. "By 2080, sea level rise could convert as much as 33 percent of the world's coastal wetlands

Flooding wiped out rice fields in Thailand in 2011. With fewer crops, Thai farmers had less rice to sell both domestically and for export.

to open water . . . a two foot [0.6 m] rise in sea level could eliminate 17–43 percent of U.S. wetlands," reported the EPA in 2009.

Flooding could have devastating effects on the farms of southern Asia. In Bangladesh nearly half of the national rice crop is grown in areas susceptible to flooding. With rising water levels and saltwater intrusion, land that was previously fertile for rice growing has already ceased to be productive. Scientists predict that Bangladeshi rice production will decrease by 20 percent by the year 2050. At the same time, summers have become longer and hotter and rainfall has become more inconsistent.

Vietnam, a nation in Southeast Asia, has encountered similar struggles. Rice farmers in the nation's Mekong Delta have seen their land and water grow saltier. Rice plants can't tolerate the salt. The world's second-largest rice exporter, Vietnam is seeking ways to develop rice that can thrive in salty water. If scientists can develop salt-tolerant rice plants, they might save their nation from an agricultural disaster.

If present trends continue, the damage to agriculture from global warming will further increase food shortages and malnutrition around the world. Climate change might even alter the landscape. In South America, places that once held tropical forests might become savanna, or

grassland. Drought and higher temperatures could also cause more forest fires. Finally, rising sea levels could damage or destroy ocean ports.
As a result, it will be difficult to transport goods, including many food
products, further exacerbating world hunger.

CHAPTER 5

FRANKENFOO

Farmers all over the globe raise genetically modified (GM) crops. This woman in India is picking cotton from a genetically modified variety of the plant.

DS

world food shortages lie in genetic engineering. Genetic engineering involves transferring deoxyribonucleic acid (DNA) from one plant or animal to another. DNA is the material that makes up genes, and genes determine which traits living things inherit from their parents.

Scientists use genetic engineering to transfer desirable traits from one organism to another. In the laboratory, they remove desired genes from a plant or an animal and insert them into the genetic material of another plant or animal. The process of genetic engineering creates organisms that are genetically slightly different from the original organisms. Plants and animals created by this process are called genetically modified organisms (GMOs).

Genetic engineering is not new. Farmers have been hybridizing (crossbreeding) plants and animals for thousands of years to create new organisms with desirable traits. Suppose a farmer wants to raise big broiler chickens, which contain a lot of meat. The farmer would pick out the largest male and female broiler chickens available and allow the two to mate. Their offspring would likely be very large chickens. The farmer could continue to mate only the largest chickens, creating bigger chickens with each new generation.

Since the twentieth century, breeding has become very high tech. With genetic engineering, modern scientists have produced crops with built-in, natural pesticides to kill harmful insects, viruses, and bacteria. Scientists have also created genetically engineered (GE) or genetically modified (GM) crops that resist herbicides. When farmers spray herbicides on their fields, the GE crops do not die along with the weeds. Some genetically engineered crops have more nutrients than ordinary crops. Others grow well in poor soil, hot climates, and periods of little rainfall. Many

agribusinesses are also developing "climate-ready" crops. These plants will be able to tolerate droughts, cold, and other stresses brought on by climate change. Still other projects are working to engineer food crops to deliver medications and vitamins to people.

The medical projects are particularly promising. For instance, the New York–based Rockefeller Foundation has created a strain of GE rice called golden rice, which is designed to prevent vitamin A deficiency. Vitamin A deficiency depresses the body's immune system and can lead to blindness. Golden rice contains carotenoids, which the body converts into vitamin A when consumed. This rice is expected to reach the market in 2012. Researchers at Cornell University in Ithaca, New York, have been working to develop GE fruit containing vaccines to protect people against hepatitis B, the measles, and other illnesses. Normally, vaccines are administered via injections. But poor nations don't always have the staff, medical facilities, or equipment necessary for injecting vaccines. In these places, it makes more sense to offer vaccines in food.

IS IT SAFE TO EAT?

An estimated two-thirds of the foodstuffs sold in the United States contain some genetically altered ingredients. For example, foods such as tomatoes, cantaloupes, soybeans, and corn commonly include genetically engineered materials. So do processed foods such as potato chips and breakfast cereals. While producers claim these foods are safe for humans to eat, around the world, consumer and environmental groups have raised concerns about GE foods. Critics say that GE foods might create future health problems in those who eat them and are

The nickname Frankenfoods (based on Frankenstein's monster, pictured above from a horror movie) sends a strong message that GE foods are not safe. But backers say the GE foods pose no health risks.

concerned that GE foods often go to market without enough safety testing. Some people have even used the name Frankenfoods to describe GE foods. The name is a play on the fictional Dr. Frankenstein, who creates a monster that he cannot control in his laboratory.

Scientists are studying possible health risks of GE foods. For example, one scientific team fed rats three types of GE corn. The scientists found evidence that the corn might be toxic to the rats. But the team cautioned: "These signs of toxicity alone do not constitute proof of adverse [negative] health effects." Other scientists are studying whether GE crops could trigger potentially deadly allergic reactions in people who eat them. Normally, people who are allergic to nuts, for instance, know to avoid this food. But what if a GE soybean contained some genetic material from a nut? Would this cause an allergic reaction? And how would

TO LABEL OR NOT?

In 1992 the FDA ruled that labels on genetically modified food were not mandatory in the United States. At the time, the FDA said that genetically modified food was no different from any other food products, except in how it was produced. The FDA left it up to producers to decide whether to label products as genetically modified or not. Most producers chose not to use the labels.

The labeling issue looms large in the twenty-first century. In a 2011 poll conducted by the *New York Times*, an overwhelming 89 percent of responders said they wanted GM food to be labeled. They believed it was their right as consumers to know what they are ingesting.

On the other side of the debate, many believe that labeling should remain voluntary. Most food producers insist that GE products are no different from their non-GE counterparts and that labeling them as genetically modified would suggest that the products are somehow inferior or potentially dangerous. Producers are also concerned about additional costs that would arise from requiring labels on GM products. Another concern is the cost of policing any labeling policy to ensure that companies are in compliance. Opponents of labeling also say that those who choose not to eat GE foods have an easy option. They can simply buy organic foods, which are labeled as such and are guaranteed not to be genetically modified.

a person who was allergic to nuts know to avoid the soybeans? Scientists and public health officials are asking these questions. Scientists continue to study possible health risks of GE food, but to date there is no concrete evidence that GE food harms humans.

GE FOR PROFIT

Opponents also worry about GE crops contaminating nonmodified crops. Winds and insects can carry pollen—tiny grains that help plants reproduce—from one field to another one far away. In this way, GE crops could cross-pollinate with and introduce unwanted traits to non-GE crops. This risk is a special concern to growers of organic crops. Organic farmers do not use any artificial pesticides, fertilizers, or other chemicals on their crops. If GE crops were to contaminate organic fields, those crops could no longer be sold as organic foods.

Monsanto researchers in Brazil inspect dead insects, killed by Roundup herbicide. The herbicide killed the insects but did not kill the soybean plants that the insects tried to feed upon.

But the biggest criticism involves giant agribusinesses using GE seeds and plants to dominate global food production for profit. Consider the case of Monsanto, the world's largest seed company. Among its many products, Monsanto sells genetically engineered soybean, canola, and corn seeds called Roundup Ready (RR) seeds. The seeds are engineered to resist Monsanto's Roundup brand of herbicide. Farmers who plant the seeds can spray Roundup directly on their fields. The herbicide will kill weeds but not the RR crops.

However, some farmers have objected strongly to RR seeds because Monsanto has a patent on them. A patent is a legal document that gives an inventor the exclusive right to make and sell an invention for a certain period of time. Other people cannot use the invention without the inventor's permission. In the past, farmers got their seeds from the crops they harvested. They owned the seeds and could plant them year after year as they wished. But that's not how it works with farmers who buy RR seeds. They must sign an agreement with Monsanto, promising to plant the seeds for only one season. If they want to plant RR seeds the following season, they must buy a new supply from Monsanto. They cannot collect seeds from the grain they grow. If farmers do collect and plant seeds from their Monsanto plants, they are violating Monsanto's patent. Monsanto even sends investigators to make sure that farmers are not illegally planting seeds. The company has sued some farmers for infringing on its patent.

In the United States, Monsanto and other big agribusinesses dominate the seed market. Smaller companies are not able to compete with them. Since the late twentieth century, many small seed firms have gone out of business. This situation leaves U.S. farmers with few choices about where to buy their seeds. They usually must buy patented seeds from a big company like Monsanto and pay high fees for new seeds each year.

The agribusinesses defend their rights to patent seeds and other farm products. They note that it costs billions of dollars each year to research and develop successful GMOs. They say they must protect their financial investments by making sure that no one uses their seeds illegally. And the companies also expect to make a profit from the sales of their seeds.

"[GE foods are a] gigantic experiment with nature and the whole of humanity which has gone seriously wrong."

—Charles, Prince of Wales, heir to the British throne and organic gardener, 2008

GE CROPS AROUND THE WORLD

Agribusinesses want to expand GE food production to poor nations worldwide. They say that farmers there can grow more crops with GE seeds and therefore help reduce hunger this way. Many African countries, faced with growing populations, hunger, and malnutrition, are "increasingly assessing a range of tools and technologies, including agricultural biotechnologies [genetic engineering], which hold great promise for improving crop yields, household incomes, and the nutritional quality of food," says Mark Rosegrant of the International Food Policy Research Institute. Rosegrant believes that GE crops that resist drought and heat will be especially beneficial for African countries, where high temperatures and little rainfall are common.

Some African farmers have already benefited from GE crops. One farmer in South Africa noted that in her community, insects frequently destroy corn plants. But the pests did not bother GE corn, which thrived. With the money she earned selling her corn, this woman could afford to expand her plantings to include tomatoes, onions, and spinach. "We were struggling to keep hunger out of our houses. Now the future looks

Egypt claims to have harvested the first crop of GE corn in the Arab world. In this photo, workers load GE corn 50 miles (80 km) outside of Cairo, the nation's capital.

good. If someone came and said we should stop using the new maize [corn], I would cry," she said.

Proponents say that high-yield genetically modified crops are needed to feed an increasing global population, estimated to total nine billion by the year 2050. But opponents are critical of businesses selling GE crops in poor nations. They say agribusinesses are interested only in profit. They can ensure huge earnings by controlling more of the agricultural market with GE seeds and by insisting that farmers buy new supplies from them year after year. The more GE seeds farmers buy, the more they will become dependent on large corporations for their agricultural needs, critics say.

Opponents also contest the argument that farmers can grow more food with GE seeds. Studies have shown that increases in world corn and soybean yields since the 1990s are chiefly due to conventional farming methods, not to GE crops. "After more than 3,000 field trials, only two types of [GE crops] are in widespread use [worldwide]," said microbiologist Margaret Mellon in 2009, "and they haven't helped raise the ceiling on potential yields."

Making matters worse, most poor farmers cannot afford GE seeds. They must buy the seeds on credit—that is, by taking out loans—and many farmers are unable to repay these loans. Stuck in an endless cycle of debt, some have become despondent and even taken their own lives. "India has experienced dramatic increases in farmer suicides caused by indebtedness for GMO seeds and chemicals," according to the Institute for Food and Development Policy.

Around the world, each country has its own rules about whether or not to allow the growth and importation of GE crops. Some nations, like the United States, have few restrictions on GE crops. Others require strict labeling, so that consumers know their foods have been genetically modified.

Restrictions on GE foods are quite strong in Europe. In 1998 the European Union banned the import of GE crops and seeds. The ban was controversial. Some people said it violated international free trade agreements. In 2004 the EU modified the ban to permit the import of GE corn seed that resists insects and herbicides, as long as the labeling made it clear that the products contained GE materials. (However, Austria, France, Greece, Germany, Luxembourg, and Hungary still ban the import of these GE seeds.) In 2010 the EU opened the door to GE crops a bit more. It approved the cultivation of a type of potato called Amflora. This potato is grown to produce industrial starch instead of food. The starch is used to make paper and other products. In 2011 the EU also agreed to allow the importation of animal feed that contained small amounts of genetically modified organisms.

GE ANIMALS

As the GE crop controversy continues, scientists have also been experimenting with genetically modified poultry, fish, and other animals. These animals could offer many benefits to growers, processors, and consumers. For instance, in the United States, researchers are genetically altering cows to produce lactose-free milk. Lactose is a milk sugar that many people cannot digest, and many people would buy lactose-free milk if it were available. U.S. scientists have also engineered chickens to resist disease, therefore cutting down on the need for poultry farmers to treat their animals with antibiotics. In addition, scientists are working on GE cattle that can resist bovine spongiform encephalopathy, also called mad cow disease. This disease not only kills cattle but also kills people who eat meat from the infected cattle.

"GM crops are safe, a crucial agricultural tool in addressing global food security, and farmers want to use them. In addition, it's a . . . fallacy [falsehood] that consumers don't want GM food."

—Matthew Cossey, chief executive officer of CropLife Australia, 2011

Using genetic engineering, scientists have also created animals with lower levels of pollutants in their wastes. An example is a genetically modified pig called the Enviropig, engineered at the University of Guelph in Ontario, Canada, in 1999. Pig manure is usually loaded with phosphorus, which often pollutes waterways. The Enviropig produces manure with little phosphorous. It is therefore less of a threat to the environment.

Scientists are genetically altering seafood as well. For example, scientists in Africa are developing genetically engineered tilapia (a freshwater fish) that grows more quickly than non-GE tilapia. With GE tilapia, fisheries will be able to get fish to market—and to hungry people in Africa—more quickly. AquaBounty Farms in eastern Prince Edward

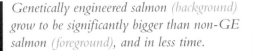
Genetically engineered salmon (background) grow to be significantly bigger than non-GE salmon (foreground), and in less time.

Island, Canada, has developed an Atlantic salmon modified with genes from Chinook salmon. Atlantic salmon usually take three years to grow large enough for market. AquaBounty's fish develop in less than half that time. The company plans to sell its salmon eggs to other fish farms in North America and awaits FDA approval to market its product in the United States. Supporters say that such projects will replenish the world's dwindling fish stocks and help feed an escalating world population.

The FDA must approve any GE livestock or fish produced commercially for food (or for any other purpose) in the United States. To date, the agency has not granted any approvals for GE food animals, and strict laws and regulations prohibit experimental GE animals from entering the food supply. According to the FDA, "The largest class of GE animals is being developed for biopharm purposes—that is, they are intended to produce substances (for example, in their milk or blood) that can be used as human or animal pharmaceuticals [prescription drugs]."

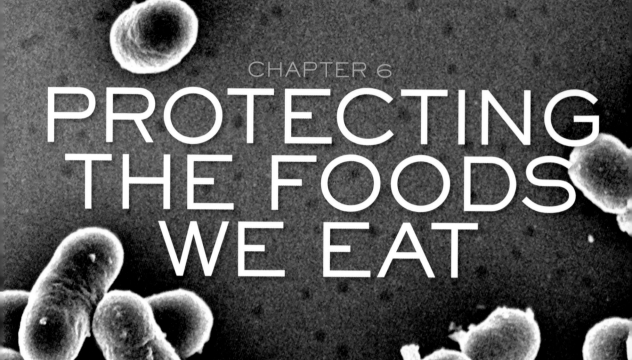

CHAPTER 6

PROTECTING THE FOODS WE EAT

This micrograph shows deadly Listeria monocytogenes, *one of many bacteria that cause foodborne illnesses in humans.*

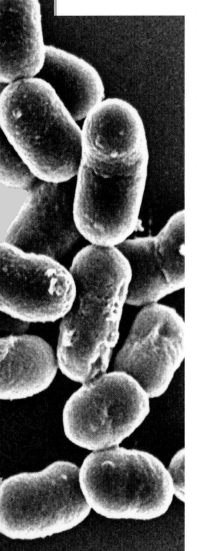

nutrients. Many people enjoy eating this healthy, tasty fruit. But in the summer of 2011, some cantaloupes became deadly. Thirty people died and 146 people fell ill after eating the fruit. Medical investigators soon found that the cantaloupes had been contaminated with *Listeria monocytogenes*, a deadly bacterium.

The FDA traced the outbreak to Jensen Farms in Colorado. The agency determined that the cantaloupes had probably been contaminated at the facility where they were stored and packed for shipment. The FDA ordered a recall to stop the spread of the *Listeria* bacteria. But it can take two months for a person to get sick after exposure to the bacteria, so people continued to get sick until November.

THE SAFETY OF U.S. FOOD

Listeria outbreaks and other foodborne illnesses cause Americans to worry about the safety of their food. In theory, the food supply should be safe. Fifteen federal government agencies oversee food safety in the United States. These agencies administer thirty different food protection laws. For instance, the USDA's Food Safety and Inspection Service inspects all raw meat sold in the United States. It ensures that beef, chicken, pork, and other meats are safe, wholesome,

"When we gather around our holiday tables, we shouldn't ever have to worry about the safety of our food. We [Americans] have the safest food supply in the world, but we can always do more to protect consumers. The best way to ensure food safety is by building prevention into our food safety system."

—Kathleen Sebelius, U.S. secretary of health and human services, 2011

and correctly labeled and packaged. The EPA enforces federal environmental laws regarding pesticide use and clean water. It monitors food hazards such as toxic pesticide residue on produce and in animal feed. The U.S. Centers for Disease Control and Prevention (CDC) investigates and monitors foodborne diseases. The FDA is responsible for regulating "80 percent of the nation's food supply, including $417 billion worth of domestic food and $49 billion in imported food annually." The FDA also enforces the Food Allergen Labeling and Consumer Protection Act of 2004. This law requires labels on food products that contain or have been in contact with any of eight major food allergens—foods that cause allergic reactions in some people. These foods are milk, eggs, fish, shellfish, tree nuts, wheat, peanuts, and soybeans. The labeling law ensures that consumers with allergies don't unknowingly eat an allergen and get sick.

The FDA says that the U.S. food supply is one of the safest in the world, but that doesn't mean it's perfect. Despite all the laws and oversight, some U.S. food does get contaminated. Each year, foodborne illness strikes 48 million Americans. Of these, roughly 128,000 need to be hospitalized and 3,000 die. The examples of foodborne illness are plentiful. In 2009, 65 people became ill with *E. coli* after eating raw Nestlé Toll House refrigerated cookie dough. As soon as investigators discovered what was making people sick, both government and business acted quickly. Working with the FDA, Nestlé immediately recalled its cookie dough. It shut down the plant where the dough was made, cleaned up its operations, and found new suppliers for its cookie dough ingredients.

The Jensen Farms, Nestlé, and other cases illustrate how difficult it is to monitor all the food production in the United States. The FDA doesn't have the funds to inspect every food processing facility. So it allows companies to hire private agencies to conduct inspections. In Jensen's case, a private company called Primus Labs inspected the facility two months before the *Listeria* outbreak. The inspection revealed a few areas where Jensen was not up to FDA safety standards, but overall Primus gave Jensen a "superior" rating for food safety. The problem areas uncovered during the inspection were not reported to the FDA.

After the *Listeria* outbreak, many lawmakers called for tighter controls over food inspection in the United States. But tighter controls will cost the government a lot of money. Some Americans, including many lawmakers, want the government to spend less money, not more. Others

This scientist in the state of Washington prepares to test bagged lettuce for E. coli. The safety of the U.S. food supply depends on thorough and regular testing such as this.

say that spending extra money on food safety should be a high priority for the U.S. government. While the politicians in Washington, D.C., debate such issues, consumers might rightly be cautious about the safety of the foods they eat.

For the most part, U.S. food companies want to sell safe food. After all, if they repeatedly sold food that sickened their customers, no one would do business with them. They would go broke. So food companies usually comply with government regulations, cooperate with inspections of their facilities, and cooperate with recalls if their food is found to be unsafe. At the same time, complying with government safety standards can be expensive. Trying to save money, some businesses are very lax about food safety. In 2009 *Salmonella*-infected peanut butter killed nine people and sickened almost seven hundred others. When government inspectors visited the business responsible for the outbreak, Peanut Corporation of America, they found cockroaches, mold, a leaking roof, and other unsanitary conditions at the facilities. The company had clearly been careless about food safety, with deadly results.

DINE OUT IN SAFETY

Many people believe that the risk of food poisoning is greater at restaurants than at home. But experts say just the opposite is true. Poor food handling practices at home pose the most risks. Restaurants train workers in food safety measures. Inspectors also visit restaurants on a regular basis to make sure they meet sanitation laws. It's still wise to observe a few basic tips when dining out:

- *Don't eat at restaurants that are obviously dirty, with overflowing garbage bins or dirty bathrooms.*

- *Be sure to order your meat, especially hamburgers, well done.*

- *If you take home leftovers, be sure to refrigerate them immediately. Eat them the next day. Otherwise, throw them out.*

Another challenge to keeping the U.S. food supply safe involves imported foods. About 15 percent of the overall U.S. food supply is imported. Sixty percent of fresh fruits and vegetables are imports, and 75 percent of seafood is imported. Imported food comes from more than 150 countries or territories and enters through more than three hundred U.S. ports. Approximately 214,000 foreign facilities manufacture or process food that is consumed in the United States, according to the FDA. U.S. agencies inspect food imports for contamination, but "as supply chains get longer and longer, there's more opportunity to introduce contaminants that have a public health effect," says former FDA official Stephen F. Sundlof. In other words, with so much imported food entering the United States, some contamination might slip by U.S. inspectors.

In January 2011, President Obama signed the Food Safety Modernization Act, which directs the FDA to build a new system of food safety oversight—one focused on applying the best available science and common sense to prevent foodborne illnesses. An important provision requires food importers to verify the safety of food from their suppliers and gives the FDA authority to block foods from facilities or countries that refuse U.S. inspection.

GLOBAL FOOD SAFETY

Many wealthy nations have food safety systems on par with that of the United States. But in poor countries, food safety programs are often inadequate or even nonexistent. Around the world, millions of people don't have access to clean water. In many nations, few people can afford refrigerators to keep food from spoiling. Governments of poor countries often cannot afford to carry out inspections, testing, and other food safety measures. As a result, worldwide, between sixty and eighty million people suffer from foodborne or waterborne illnesses each year. These illnesses cause approximately six to eight million deaths annually.

As the world becomes more industrialized, keeping food safe becomes even harder. Food processors routinely add coloring, thickeners, and preservatives to foods to make them more appetizing or to keep them from spoiling. In most cases, such additives are safe to eat, but on occasion, additives have made people sick. One of the most frightening food safety crises occurred in China in the fall of 2008. Inspections of Chinese infant formula and other dairy items revealed that these products were contaminated with melamine, an industrial chemical. Chinese food processors had deliberately used the chemical as filler in dairy foods.

Parents in eastern China wait at a hospital with their children in 2008. The babies were tested to make sure they hadn't ingested melamine, an industrial chemical, through dairy items.

FYI

The FDA posts a database of food recalls at http://www.fda.gov/opacom/7alerts.html. You can search the database by brand name or product type to see if any of the foods you and your family eat are on this list.

The Chinese government reported that fifty-three thousand infants became sick and four died after drinking tainted formula. The products had also been shipped to nations around the globe, and some illegal shipments might have reached the United States. The FDA warned American consumers to avoid the Chinese formula and emphasized that no dairy products manufactured in the United States were contaminated.

FOOD DISASTERS

In the spring of 2010, an oil rig exploded in the Gulf of Mexico, part of the Atlantic Ocean. The explosion damaged an undersea oil well, which leaked more than 185 million gallons (700 million liters) of oil into the Gulf. The oil sickened and killed plants and animals living in the water and on lands along the shore. In response to the crisis, the FDA and other federal and state government agencies banned the harvesting of seafood, including fish, shrimp, crabs, and oysters, from certain Gulf waters. People worried that seafood from the Gulf would be contaminated with oil—and they didn't want to eat it. The ban was economically difficult for Gulf Coast commercial fishers, seafood distributors, and restaurants that served seafood meals. In 2011, after the leak was sealed and the oil began to dissipate, or break up, government inspectors conducted extensive testing of seafood from the Gulf. Tests showed that seafood from most of the Gulf is as safe to eat as it was before the oil spill, according to an April 2011 report from the FDA. A few waters remain closed to seafood harvesting, however.

Another threat to food safety occurred in March 2011, when a powerful earthquake struck off the coast of Japan. The quake caused a tsunami, or giant wave, that disabled a Japanese nuclear power plant. The plant leaked deadly radioactive particles into the air and water. Farmland and fisheries near the plant were contaminated. Fearing that

Radiation testing centers were set up in Japan after the nuclear meltdown there in 2011. This woman brings bags of cabbage and rice for testing.

"Some areas still have high radiation dosages and if you also eat products from these areas, you'll get a considerable amount of radiation. "This is why the government needs to do something fast."

—Sentaro Takahashi, professor, Kyoto University, several months after the Japanese nuclear disaster, 2011

crops and seafood from Japan would be unhealthy to eat, the United States, Canada, Australia, and other nations increased their inspection of food imports from Japan. According to the U.S. Congressional Research Service, the Japanese government "has taken steps to monitor and restrict, if necessary, the distribution of contaminated foods." And since the tragedy, "testing has been conducted nearly daily to detect possible radioactive contaminants on a wide range of plant and animal products, including fish." Critics say that the Japanese testing efforts are inadequate, however. They say the government is doing only minimal testing in a small area around the damaged nuclear plant and that contamination of Japanese food is far more widespread than the government has admitted.

The disasters in the Gulf of Mexico and Japan are extreme cases of contaminants entering the food supply. But disasters aside, the everyday pollution of water, air, and soil is an ongoing worry for food safety. Industries such as mining and manufacturing sometimes dump hazardous metals and chemicals into waterways, where they can contaminate food supplies. As industrial growth continues, it might take new laws and new technologies to keep our food sources safe for future generations.

CHAPTER 7

FOOD MEETS POLITICS

The U.S. government wants to make school lunches more nutritious. Healthy eating includes more fresh fruits and vegetables and less sugar, salt, and starch in each meal.

part of the day. It offers a break from teachers and classes and gives kids a chance to spend fun time with friends. The nation's school lunch program, administered by the USDA, helps ensure that U.S. kids don't go hungry. The program provides meals to more than 30.5 million schoolchildren, most of whom come from families that cannot afford school lunches.

The USDA wants to make sure that lunches provided through the school lunch program are nutritious. It works with doctors, scientists, and nutritionists to set rules about how much and what types of food are included in lunches. In 2011 the USDA, operating on recommendations from a nonprofit agency called the Institute of Medicine, proposed changes in the school lunch system that would increase nutritional standards. The USDA wanted to lessen the amount of starch, sugars, and sodium served in school lunches, since these substances contribute to childhood obesity. As part of the proposal, the USDA wanted to decrease starch in children's diets by cutting the amount of french fries served in the school lunch program.

Large food corporations fought against the proposal. These companies make millions of dollars a year by supplying food to the school lunch program. If the USDA limited the amount of french fries in school lunches, for instance, the suppliers of frozen potatoes would lose a lot of money. Agribusinesses pressured the U.S. Congress to reject the USDA's proposal. In the end, Congress approved a watered-down version of the proposed guidelines. The new regulations called for less sodium in lunches, but the number of potato servings was not decreased. Nutritionists were disappointed with the final regulations.

The fight over school lunches illustrates the intersection of food and politics. This crossroads is often further intersected by money. When the federal and state governments purchase foods for various programs, such as school lunches, they spend a great deal of money. For example, the USDA buys more than 60 million pounds (27 million kg) of chicken products for school lunches and other nutrition programs each year, at a cost of about $42.2 million. The big winners in this deal are the chicken processors Pilgrim's Pride and Tyson, which provide most of this chicken to the government.

> *"Clearly more pizza and French fries in schools is not good for kids, but it's good for companies that make pizza and French fries."*
>
> —Margo Wootan, Center for Science in the Public Interest, 2011

AGRICULTURAL LOBBYISTS

To win and keep such big government contracts, beef and pork producers, frozen food companies, fresh produce associations, snack food and breakfast cereal companies, food importers, and other food businesses send representatives to Washington, D.C., and to state capitals. These representatives lobby (try to influence) government officials, encouraging them to pass laws favorable to their industries.

One agricultural trade group, the Mid America CropLife Association (MACA), represents agribusinesses that produce chemical fertilizers and pesticides. These businesses include Dow AgroSciences, Monsanto, and DuPont. After First Lady Michelle Obama and fifth graders planted a kitchen garden outside the White House in 2009, the MACA became concerned. The garden is organic, so the gardeners use no chemical pesticides or fertilizers on the plants. The group sent a letter to Michelle Obama, complimenting her for highlighting farming by growing vegetables and fruits. But the letter went on to promote conventional agriculture. It said the nation had produced "the safest and most abundant food supply in the world thanks to the 3 million people who farm or ranch in the United States." The letter then noted:

> *We live in a very different world than that of our grandparents. . . . The*

First Lady Michelle Obama and helpers harvest vegetables from the White House organic garden. One of the First Lady's missions is to teach kids about food, nutrition, and healthy eating.

time needed to tend a garden is not there for the majority of our citizens, certainly not a garden of sufficient productivity to supply much of a family's year-round food needs. . . . As you go about planning and planting the White House garden, we respectfully encourage you to recognize the role conventional agriculture plays in the U.S in feeding the ever-increasing population, contributing to the U.S. economy and providing a safe and economical food supply.

An organic garden at the White House, the MACA argued, gave the impression that conventionally grown food—food grown with the aid of chemicals—is somehow harmful. (The White House did not respond to the letter.) The MACA letter is only one effort—and a small one at that—to try to impact the nation's agricultural policies. But other efforts are much larger.

FARM SUBSIDIES

The U.S. government provides many benefits for large-scale food producers. Agribusiness receives the biggest share of federal agricultural subsidies. Subsidies are tax breaks and government money given to farmers. The government provides farm subsidies to keep the U.S. farming industry healthy and to assure a strong national and global food supply. Subsidies help farmers in downtimes, such as when pests or bad weather wipe out their crops, or when crop prices fall. The government provides subsidies for a range of farm products, such as grain, sugarcane, dairy foods, and cotton.

Every five years, the U.S. Congress revises the Food, Conservation, and Energy Act, nicknamed the Farm Bill. The bill addresses agriculture and food policy in the United States. Part of the Farm Bill includes a $44 billion agricultural subsidy to farmers. Most of the money goes to large industrialized farms, while family farms receive only a small portion.

Critics of agricultural subsidies argue that individual farmworkers and other laborers do not get financial help from the U.S. government, so why should farm owners? Critics would especially like to limit the subsidies that go to large agribusinesses. These businesses already make large profits and therefore don't need government assistance. Opponents further note that large-scale agriculture has forced many family farms out of business, since small farmers can't compete with massive farm operations using assembly-line techniques and other economies of scale. They ask: is it fair to hand out money to big businesses when small businesses struggle to survive?

Some critics say that farm subsidies also damage the environment. The subsidies encourage monoculture—the growing of a single crop on a large piece of land. Monoculture quickly pulls nutrients from the soil and does not replenish them. Thus crops require huge amounts of fertilizer, which can run off and pollute water supplies.

> *"Around the world [people in] some countries spend 60 to 80 percent of their income on food. In the U.S., we spend closer to 10 percent. Without those [farm] subsidies, it would cost the consumer a whole lot more to buy the food they get."*
>
> *—David Carter, county agricultural agent, Natchez, Mississippi, 2010*

In addition, farm subsidies encourage large-scale farming in dry areas, which are more suitable for livestock grazing. Farms in dry regions require huge amounts of water for irrigation, diverting water from other uses, such as drinking supplies.

But many people support farm subsidies. They point out that because of unpredictable changes in weather and the economy, growers cannot count on a steady income from the crops they produce and sell. Prices for crops may spike or drop dramatically from year to year. Weather conditions, such as droughts and floods, can also hurt agricultural production and farm income. Many U.S. farms would be unable to survive without subsidies, supporters say. Supporters further argue that farm subsidies assure that Americans will be well fed, for fairly low prices, and not overly dependent on food imports.

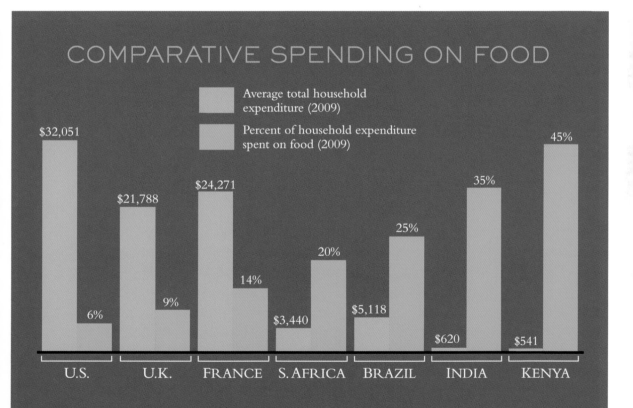

COMPARATIVE SPENDING ON FOOD

■ Average total household expenditure (2009)
■ Percent of household expenditure spent on food (2009)

	U.S.	U.K.	FRANCE	S. AFRICA	BRAZIL	INDIA	KENYA
Expenditure	$32,051	$21,788	$24,271	$3,440	$5,118	$620	$541
Percent on food	6%	9%	14%	20%	25%	35%	45%

Americans spend less of their household income on food than people in any other nation. Some people say that farm subsidies are responsible for keeping U.S. food prices low.

THE LONG JOURNEY FOR U.S. FOOD AID

Food aid from the United States to nations overseas often moves very slowly. Consider one shipment: bags of dried green peas traveling from North Dakota to starving people in the small African village of Shala-Luka, Ethiopia, during a drought. The shipment was arranged by USAID and the USDA.

The shipment began its 12,000-mile (19,300-kilometer) journey in Minot, North Dakota. There, a Minot farmer sold his spring crop of peas to a broker, or sales agent. The broker stored the peas in a warehouse. Then a train carried the peas 1,800 miles (2,896 km) to Lake Charles, Louisiana, where the peas again sat in a warehouse. In early July, workers loaded the peas onto a cargo ship called the *John A. Chapman*. It took about six weeks for the ship to cross the Atlantic Ocean and reach port in the east African country of Djibouti. From there, the shipment of peas went to Nazareth, Ethiopia. The peas again sat in a warehouse, until they finally traveled by truck to Shala-Luka. By the time the food reached the village in October, more than six months after the journey began, several children and adults in one Shala-Luka family had died of starvation.

This example is not unique. Most U.S. aid shipments take between four and six months to reach the needy. Why does the food move so slowly? The answer involves laws regarding U.S. food aid, which require that almost all food aid shipments come from U.S. sources. The law also requires that 75 percent of U.S. food aid be transported by U.S. shipping companies.

Critics say it would be more efficient and less costly to buy food from sources closer to areas of need. They say USAID funds should go to agencies already working in impoverished regions of the world. These agencies could then purchase local food and greatly cut transportation costs. Critics also attack the requirement that U.S. shippers transport most U.S. food aid. This requirement, critics note, means that giant agribusinesses, grain processors, railroads, trucking companies, and shipping companies all make money off the hunger of poor people. Some critics have tried to revise the laws regarding U.S. food aid. But U.S. farm organizations and corporations want to protect their profits. They have successfully lobbied Congress to keep the laws in place.

FOOD AS A WEAPON

Americans generally think of food as a wonderful treat. But in some parts of the world, governments sometimes use food as a weapon. For instance, during wartime, governments might provide food to reward people for loyalty. They might deliberately withhold food to destroy opponents. Throughout history, dictators and conquerors have used a variety of methods to destroy enemy food supplies, such as contaminating farmland so that crops cannot grow, burning grain fields, stopping shipments of food aid to starving people, and even poisoning food.

In the twenty-first century, dictator Robert Mugabe, president of the African nation of Zimbabwe, has used food as a weapon against his own people. In 2008 Zimbabwe suffered a severe drought that devastated crops. The World Food Programme and other relief agencies tried to ship food to help the nation's starving people. Mugabe banned the shipments, because he claimed that the aid agencies supported his political opponents, the Movement for Democratic Change (MDC). MDC

Millions of children around the world suffer from malnutrition. Here, three boys pick through garbage at a dump in the eastern African nation of Somalia, hoping to find scraps of food.

leader Morgan Tsvangirai and relief agency officials accused Mugabe of deliberately starving his people to stay in power. Tsvangirai ran for president in 2008 but lost the election. Months of violence followed. Eventually, Mugabe and Tsvangirai made a power-sharing agreement, by which Mugabe serves as president and Tsvangirai as prime minister. The two leaders have since allowed more food shipments into Zimbabwe, but critics charge that Mugabe still routinely distributes food supplies to his supporters and withholds them from his opponents.

Food politics has taken a big toll in Somalia, the site of many famines. In 2009 a militant Islamic group, al-Shabaab, refused to allow food aid shipments into Somali regions under its control. Al-Shabaab blocked the shipments because much of the food came from the United States and Europe, which al-Shabaab viewed as its enemy. In 2011 aid groups began partnering with Islamic countries and organizations to deliver food to Somalia, by then suffering from severe drought and famine. Al-Shabaab was less hostile to its Islamic neighbors and allowed the food to be distributed.

A woman sits near a UN food shipment in northern Pakistan in 2009. After a suicide bombing in the region, some aid agencies stopped food distribution there, fearing for workers' safety.

The United States has also withheld food from certain nations in an effort to persuade repressive governments to change their policies. The hope is that government leaders will change course rather than see their people go hungry. For example, in 1990, the United States and other nations refused to do business with Iraq. The embargo, or ban on commerce, included most food shipments. The international community was trying to pressure the Iraqi dictator Saddam Hussein to rid his country of suspected weapons of mass destruction, including biological and chemical weapons. Instead of changing Iraqi policy, however, the embargo ultimately led to food shortages and hunger for the poorest people of Iraq.

To alleviate this suffering, the United Nations developed a program called Oil for Food in 1995. Under this program, Iraq was allowed to sell its valuable oil to earn money to feed its people. The program was beset by corruption, however. Although a lot of money from the sale of oil did go to provide food to the Iraqi people, Saddam Hussein also ended up siphoning off a great deal of the oil money for himself.

FEEDING THE FUTURE

Eating food is one of the most pleasurable things that friends and family do together. Making sure that global citizens have enough safe food to eat and that farmers produce it in a healthy, safe way are important goals in the twenty-first century.

that would provide adequate nutrients for people worldwide and get rid of world hunger? Scientists say it is theoretically possible to create food in pill form, but people are unlikely to want such a pill. Most people want the satisfaction of tasting and enjoying food. They find great pleasure in socializing while they eat—meeting with family, friends, classmates, coworkers, and others around a meal or snacks.

Many people think that industrial food production, including factory farms and genetically modified crops and animals, is the best way to produce the food that people need and want. Supporters say it is the only practical and economical way to provide food for billions of people around the world. They note that because of industrial farming practices, U.S. food production has increased dramatically since the late nineteenth century. Proponents also say that industrialized agriculture has given consumers a wide variety of high-quality food choices.

But many others around the globe are challenging the industrial farming system for its use of pesticides, fertilizers, herbicides, hormones, antibiotics, GMO seeds, and GE practices. They call for an alternative system of agriculture to guarantee a healthy, locally based, environmentally safe, and generous food supply for generations to come. This system, called sustainable agriculture, would treat farmworkers and consumers fairly and honestly.

WHAT IS SUSTAINABLE AGRICULTURE?

The word *sustain* means "keep in existence" or "maintain." When applied to agriculture, *sustainable* describes a farming system that can be productive indefinitely. A report from the University of California–Davis, explained this principle.

Sustainability rests on the principle that we must meet the needs of the present without compromising the ability of future generations to meet their own needs. Therefore, stewardship of both natural and human resources is of prime importance. Stewardship of human resources includes consideration of social responsibilities such as working and living conditions of laborers, the needs of rural communities, and consumer health and safety both in the present and the future. Stewardship of land and natural resources involves maintaining or enhancing this vital resource base for the long term.

EATING INSECTS?

One suggestion for increasing a sustainable food supply comes from entomophagists. These people encourage cooking and eating insects, such as ants, caterpillars, crickets, grasshoppers, spiders, and water bugs. Experts say insects are a source of protein and other nutrients and are a sustainable food source. Actually, this is not a new idea. People already eat insects in Japan, Mexico, Papua New Guinea, Thailand, and many African nations. But in the United States, deep-fried crickets and grasshoppers *(below)* do not attract a lot of diners. Deep-fried insects are popular in Thailand, China, and other parts of Asia.

Sustainable agriculture challenges food growers and producers to balance the long-term environmental effects of their farming or ranching practices with the need to earn a living. With a sustainable agriculture system, farmers would protect groundwater and streams from contamination by livestock waste and agricultural chemicals. They would nurture the soil and keep it healthy to ensure long-term productivity.

Crop rotation is an important part of sustainable agriculture. Many conventional farmers use monoculture. They plant a single crop, such as corn, year after year. But corn uses up the nitrogen in soil. Farmers who practice sustainable agriculture, by contrast, might grow corn in a field one year and alfalfa or soybeans in the same field the next. Alfalfa and soybeans help restore nitrogen to the soil. After harvesting, a farmer might then plant cover crops such as rye, clover, or vetch (a vinelike plant). These plants also improve the quality of soil. Their roots hold the soil together, so it doesn't become loose and blow away in the wind.

Sustainable agriculture might also involve integrated pest management (IPM). IPM involves killing agricultural pests with their own natural enemies instead of with chemical pesticides. For instance, ladybugs and their larvae (insects in their wormlike stage) feed on lice that can kill food crops. Some farmers release ladybugs into their fields to attack harmful pests.

Sustainable agriculture recognizes that farmed land is an ecosystem—a system of plants, animals, and other organisms that interact as a unit. By keeping the system in balance, farmers can ensure that they produce healthy food for long periods of time without relying on industrial-made chemicals and other products that harm the environment and pose risks to human health.

Some farmers rely on two-spotted ladybugs such as these to naturally control crop-destroying pests. These ladybugs feast on aphids (the small white bugs on the leaf).

SUSTAINABILITY EFFORTS

An increasing number of environmental groups, food aid agencies, farmers, and political organizations are joining forces to encourage sustainable farming practices. Slow Food International, for example, is a social and political movement with more than one hundred thousand members in more than 150 countries. The movement encourages consumers to forgo fast food and industrialized food production and to enjoy locally and sustainably grown foods.

The locavore movement encourages people to eat only locally grown foods. In the United States, most food travels hundreds and even thousands of miles from its source to supermarket shelves. Shipping all that food by truck, boat, or train creates a lot of greenhouse gases. By eating locally, people can reduce greenhouse gas emissions. They also support the local economy and enjoy fresher foods—much of it harvested only days before.

On an individual basis, people who want to avoid mass-produced food can grow their own produce, even if they have only a small plot of urban ground for that purpose. Some individuals are turning entire urban lawns into edible gardens. One family in Pasadena, California, plants

Buying food at a farmers' market is one way to support local, sustainable, and organic farming in your area. This woman buys fresh herbs at a market in Virginia.

all the space around their home with organic fruits and vegetables. They harvest enough produce to feed themselves, and they sell the rest.

Many schools are also jumping into organic gardening. The Edible Schoolyard program was started by renowned chef and restaurant owner Alice Waters in 1995. Working with the Martin Luther King Jr. Middle School in Berkeley, California, she created a 1-acre (0.4-hectare) garden for the school's students. The students planted organic vegetables, tended them as they grew, harvested them, and then made meals from the produce. They also learned about sustainable agriculture and nutrition. The Edible Schoolyard program has since expanded to cities across the United States.

ORGANIC FARMING

Joel Salatin, featured in the 2009 documentary *Food, Inc.*, grows organic foods on his 550-acre (223-hectare) Polyface Farm in Virginia's Shenandoah Valley. The family farm operates without the use of commercial fertilizers, seeds, pesticides, or herbicides. It produces thousands of broiler chickens and hundreds of thousands of eggs, cattle, pigs, rabbits, and turkeys. Cattle on the farm move to a different pasture each day, eating the plants there and receiving no grain, antibiotics, or growth hormones.

FOOD IN THE FOREST

Instead of going to the supermarket for fresh nuts, fruits, and berries, people in Seattle, Washington, have a new option. In the summer of 2012, city gardeners created a "food forest" in Seattle's Beacon Hill neighborhood. The 7-acre (2.8-hectare) plot of land is planted with walnut and chestnut trees, blueberry and raspberry bushes, fruit trees, herbs, and more. Best of all for city residents, all the food that grows in the forest is free for the taking.

Polyface Farm is one of more than twenty thousand U.S. farms engaged in organic production. To be certified as organic, farms must abide by strict guidelines. Here is how the USDA defines organic food:

Organic food is produced by farmers who emphasize the use of renewable resources and the conservation of soil and water to enhance environmental quality for future generations. Organic meat, poultry, eggs, and dairy products come from animals that are given no antibiotics or growth hormones. Organic food is produced without using most conventional pesticides; fertilizers made with synthetic ingredients or sewage sludge; bioengineering [genetic modification]; or . . . radiation. Before a product can be labeled "organic," a Government-approved certifier inspects the farm where the food is grown to make sure the farmer is following all the rules necessary to meet USDA organic standards.

Many consumers prefer organically grown food to conventionally grown food. Many natural foods supermarkets offer organic produce alongside conventional produce. Even giant retailer Walmart sells some organic foods in its grocery aisles. The organic food movement has also spread across the globe—from Asia to South America. In 2009, 92 million acres (37.2 million hectares) of farmland worldwide were devoted

Joel Salatin is one of many organic farmers in the United States. Among other things, he raises chickens on his farm in Virginia. He does not contain the poultry in crowded containment facilities, allowing the chickens to roam outdoors instead.

> "The single greatest lesson the garden teaches is that our relationship to the planet need not be sum-zero, and that as long as the sun still shines and people can still plan and plant, think and do, we can, if we bother to try, find ways to provide for ourselves without diminishing the world."
>
> —*Michael Pollan, food writer, 2008*

to producing organic food. Australia had the most farmland (30 million acres, or 12 million hectares) under organic cultivation, followed by Argentina (10.9 million acres, or 4.4 million hectares) and the United States (4.7 million acres, or 1.9 million hectares).

THE FOOD CRISIS CONTINUES

While debates continue about ways to feed the world's population, the food crisis in poor nations is by no means near resolution. Food is the new gold, and in many areas of the world, obtaining it is still like finding treasure. By 2050 an estimated 2.7 billion people will be added to the world's population, increasing the demand for grains, fish, and other food.

Will future food systems be able to supply the demand? Will industrialized food production systems dominate in the future, or will alternative, sustainable methods make inroads? Some experts believe that a combination of both systems may be needed. "It is unrealistic to assume that one grand plan—one magic bullet—will solve all the world's food problems. Each person, each region, each country, will have a different set of circumstances to consider when choosing the direction they wish to follow," write Andrew Heintzman and Evan Solomon, editors of the book *Feeding the Future*.

In the United States and other wealthy countries, activism, legislation, and government programs will influence the direction of food production. But ultimately, consumers will play a significant role. By carefully considering what food they buy; where they buy it; and the environmental, social, and health impacts of their choices, consumers will help determine how and what food is produced in the years ahead.

GLOSSARY

AGRIBUSINESS: large-scale corporate farming and all the businesses that support it, including seed production; livestock breeding; the growing and harvesting of crops; and the processing, distribution, marketing, and sales of the final products

AGRICULTURAL SUBSIDIES: grants of government money and tax breaks for farmers

ANTIBIOTIC: a medication that can kill certain disease-causing organisms

BIOFUEL: fuel produced from plant products or from vegetable oils. Ethanol is a common biofuel made by fermenting the sugars in sugarcane or corn.

RECOMBINANT BOVINE GROWTH HORMONE (RBGH): an artificial growth hormone that farmers inject into cows to increase the animals' milk production

CARBON DIOXIDE: one of several naturally occurring greenhouse gases in Earth's atmosphere. Increasing levels of carbon dioxide in the atmosphere, caused by the burning of fossil fuels, are causing Earth to grow warmer.

CLIMATE CHANGE: the warming of Earth over time due to increasing levels of greenhouse gases in the atmosphere

CONCENTRATED ANIMAL FEEDING OPERATION (CAFO): a livestock business that concentrates large numbers of animals in relatively small and confined places. At CAFOs, employees use high-tech equipment to feed animals, control room temperatures, administer medicines, and manage animal waste.

CROP ROTATION: planting a field with different crops from year to year to restore nutrients to the soil

CROSSBREED: to breed different varieties of a plant or animal to obtain desirable features in the offspring

DROUGHT: a long period with little or no rainfall

ECONOMY OF SCALE: a reduction in the cost of producing something brought about by increasing the size of a facility and the number of units it can produce

FACTORY FARMS: giant farming operations that use assembly-line techniques to breed, grow, slaughter, and process animals for food. Large numbers of animals are kept in huge facilities and are not allowed to graze. Meat, milk, and eggs are the main products of factory farms.

FERTILIZERS: substances, such as manure or chemicals, that farmers apply to cropland to add nutrients to the soil so that plants will thrive

FIELD FACTORIES: giant farms that hire large numbers of migrant workers to plant and harvest fruits and vegetables

FOOD INSECURITY: when people do not have enough safe, nutritious food to lead a healthy, active life

FOSSIL FUELS: carbon-based fuels formed naturally deep underground from the remains of long-dead plants and animals. Coal, oil, and natural gas are examples of fossil fuels.

GENETICALLY MODIFIED ORGANISM (GMO): a plant or animal whose traits have been changed by genetic engineering

GENETIC ENGINEERING (GE): altering the genes of an organism to change the organism's characteristics. This form of biotechnology is commonly used in modern research, agriculture, and medicine.

GLOBAL WARMING: the warming of Earth's climate due to increased levels of greenhouse gases, especially carbon dioxide, in the atmosphere. Most scientists believe that the burning of large amounts of fossil fuels has caused global warming. Scientists predict that global warming will bring more droughts, rising sea levels, and more extreme weather to Earth.

GREENHOUSE EFFECT: the natural process by which Earth's atmosphere traps heat from the sun, helping keep Earth warm. The burning of fossil fuels in large amounts has increased this process, causing Earth's climate to warm.

GREENHOUSE GAS: a gas, such as carbon dioxide, that traps heat from the sun, preventing it from escaping out of Earth's atmosphere and back out into space

GREEN REVOLUTION: beginning after World War II, a great increase in worldwide agricultural production as a result of the introduction of high-yielding grain varieties, broader distribution of hybrid seeds, greater use of pesticides and fertilizers, expansion of irrigation, and more efficient farm management techniques

HERBICIDE: a substance, such as a chemical spray, that farmers apply to agricultural fields to destroy weeds

INDUSTRIALIZATION: the switch from human- or animal-powered labor to labor carried out by power-driven machinery, vehicles, and other technology

INTEGRATED PEST MANAGEMENT (IPM): a method of killing insects and other pests that relies on the animals' natural enemies instead of chemical pesticides. For instance, some farmers release ladybugs into their fields. The ladybugs feed on certain pests that kill tomato, cabbage, broccoli, and other plants.

IRRIGATION: a system of channels, reservoirs, and machines for carrying water to farm fields

LIVESTOCK: cattle, sheep, goats, swine (pigs), poultry, and other animals used as food for humans

LOBBY: to try to persuade public officials to either pass or vote against laws or policies that favor or hurt a particular group. Most U.S. industries, such as agribusiness, send lobbyists to Washington, D.C., to pressure U.S. senators and representatives to vote for or against certain laws.

LOCAVORE MOVEMENT: an organized effort to encourage people to produce, purchase, and eat locally grown food as a way to cut down on long-distance shipping, thereby reducing shipping costs as well as the burning of fossil fuels

MALNUTRITION: a condition in which the body doesn't get enough vitamins, minerals, and other nutrients for healthy living. Malnutrition is a result of not getting enough food, eating too much food, or not eating a healthy balance of foods.

MIGRANT WORKER: a laborer who travels from farm to farm to plant and harvest crops each season

MONOCULTURE: the growth of a single crop on vast areas of land year after year. This type of farming is typical of industrialized farming. It allows for larger yields but at the same time uses up nutrients in soil and makes crops more likely to be hit by plant diseases and pests.

NUTRIENTS: a naturally or technologically produced chemical that allows for the growth of living things

ORGANIC FARMING: growing crops and raising livestock without artificial fertilizers, pesticides, herbicides, antibiotics, growth hormones, or genetically modified seeds

PESTICIDES: substances, such as poisonous chemicals, that farmers use to kill insects and other pests that harm crops

SLOW FOOD MOVEMENT: an international social and political movement that encourages consumers to forgo fast food and industrialized food production and to enjoy locally and sustainably grown foods

SUSTAINABLE AGRICULTURE: a system and philosophy of farming based on meeting human food needs in a way that is respectful of the environment, people, plants, and animals and that can be maintained in the long run without damaging or depleting natural resources

SOURCE NOTES

5. James Chapman, "Summit That's Hard to Swallow," *Daily Mail* (London), July 8, 2008, http://www.dailymail.co.uk/news/worldnews/article-1032909/Summit-thats-hard-swallow-world-leaders-enjoy-18-course-banquet-discuss-solve-global-food-crisis.html# (January 19, 2009).

10. International Fund for Agricultural Development, "A Loan, a Lamb and a Livelihood in Tunisia," *Rural Poverty Portal*, n.d., http://www.ruralpovertyportal.org/web/guest/country/voice/tags/tunisia/livelihood# (May 16, 2009).

10. International Fund for Agricultural Development, "Liquid Gold Helps Eritrean Farmers Defy the Looming Threat of Drought," *IFAD*, n.d., http://operations.ifad.org/web/guest/country/voice/tags/eritrea/eritreahoney# (May 16, 2009).

14. Kimberley Chin and Kevin McGuire, "A Food Stamp Challenge That We All Can Help With," *Washington Post*, August 3, 2008, B08.

14. Congressional Food Stamp Challenge, "U.S. Members of Congress Live on a Food Stamp Budget," *Congressional Food Stamp Challenge*, June 2007, http://foodstampchallenge.typepad.com/ (January 18, 2009).

14. George A. Jones, "Hunger and Obesity," *Beyond Bread*, January 5, 2009, http://breadforthecity.blogspot.com/2009/01/letter-to-editor-hunger-and-obesity.html (May 11, 2009).

10. UN News Service, "On World Food Day, UN Agencies Urge Concerted Effort against Global Hunger," *UN News Center*, 2011, http://www.un.org/apps/news/story.asp?NewsID=40058&Cr=hunger&Cr1= (February 4, 2012).

17. Michael Pollan, *Food Inc,*—Official Trailer [HD] Video, ovguide.com , 2009 ,http://www.ovguide.com/video/food-inc-official-trailer-hd-922ca39ce10036ba0e115 4f162339791 (March 28, 2012).

23. Blake Hurst, "The Omnivore's Delusion," *American*, July 30, 2009, http://www.american.com/archive/2009/july/the-omnivore2019s-delusion-against-the-agri-intellectuals (February 26, 2012).

25. Humane Farming Association, "HFA's National Veal Boycott," *HFA*, n.d., http://www.hfa.org/campaigns/boycott.html (February 2, 2009).

26. American Veal Industry, "Facts about the Care and Feeding of Calves," *American Veal Industry*, n.d., http://www.vealfarm.com/edu-resources/downloads/calf-care.pdf (February 2, 2009).

27. Charlie LeDuff, "At a Slaughterhouse, Some Things Never Die," *New York Times*, June 16, 2000, http://www.nytimes.com/library/national/race/061600leduff-meat.html (February 17, 2009).

28. Congressional Research Service, "Labor Practices in the Meat Packing and Poultry Processing Industry: An Overview," *National Agriculture Law Center*, October 27, 2006, http://www.nationalaglawcenter.org/assets/crs/RL33002.pdf (February 5, 2009).

28. Human Rights Watch, "Blood, Sweat, and Fear," *Human Rights Watch*, January 24, 2005, http://www.hrw.org/en/node/11869/section/1 (February 6, 2009).

29. Human Rights Watch, "Blood, Sweat, and Fear."

30. Anu K. Mittal, "Concentrated Animal Feeding Operations EPA Needs More Information and a Clearly Defined Strategy to Protect Air and Water Quality," *Government Accountability Office*, September 24, 2008, http://www.gao.gov/new.items

/d081177t.pdf (February 17, 2009).

31. John Carlin, "Putting Meat on the Table: Industrial Farm Animal Production in America," *Pew Charitable Trusts and Johns Hopkins Bloomberg School of Public Health*, 2008, http://www.pewtrusts.org/uploadedFiles/wwwpewtrustsorg/Reports /Industrial_Agriculture/PCIFAP_FINAL.pdf (May 30, 2009).

30. Michael Greger, "Reasons to End Factory Farming," *Organic Portal*, 2011, http://www .organicportal.info/index.php/home-mainmenu-1/news-mainmenu-2/1-latest/2177- news-reasons-to-end-factory-farming.html (February 4, 2012).

36. Meg Gaige, "In Defense of Dairy CAFOs," *Flakes Community Forum*, May 15, 2008, http://flakes1.wordpress.com/2008/05/15/guest-opinion-in-defense-of-dairy-cafos/ (February 26, 2012).

40. Intergovernmental Panel on Climate Change, "Climate Change 2007: Synthesis Report Summary for Policymakers," *IPCC*, 2007, http://www.ipcc.ch/pdf /assessment-report/ar4/syr/ar4_syr_spm.pdf (February 19, 2009).

41. Elizabeth Kolbert, "Outlook: Extreme," *National Geographic*, April 2009, 60.

41. United Nations, "Majority of World Population Face Water Shortages Unless Action Taken, Warns Migiro," *United Nations News Centre*, February 5, 2009, http://www .un.org/apps/news/story.asp?NewsID=29796&Cr=water&Cr1=agriculture# (February 23, 2009).

42–43. Alex Morales, "Greenland and Antarctica Glaciers Speeding Faster Toward the Sea," *Bloomberg.com*, February 26, 2009, http://www.bloomberg.com/apps/news?pid= 20601085&sid=aTg9EF2NtBCg&refer=europe# (February 28, 2009).

45–46. United States Environmental Protection Agency, "Coastal Zones and Sea Level Rise," *EPA*, February 20, 2009, http://www.epa.gov/climatechange/effects/coastal/index .html (May 18, 2009).

43. Notable Quotes, "Quotes on Global Warming," *Notable Quotes.com*, 2005, http:// www.notable-quotes.com/g/global_warming_quotes.html (February 23, 2009).

51. Joël Spiroux de Vendômois, François Roullier, Dominique Cellier, and Gilles-Eric Séralini, "A Comparison of the Effects of Three GM Corn Varieties on Mammalian Health," *International Journal of Biological Science*, 2009, http://www.biolsci.org /v05p0706.htm (January 24, 2010).

54. Michele Pietrowski, "Researchers, Policymakers Convene Conference to Discuss the Implications of GM Crops for Smallholder African Farmers," *International Food Policy Research Institute*, May 19, 2009, http://www.ifpri.org/PRESSREL/2009 /pressrel20090519.pdf (August 13, 2009).

54–55. Paul Driessen and Cyril Boynes Jr., "Facts vs. Fears on Biotechnology: Misplaced Opposition to GM Crops Violates Poor People's Basic Human Rights," *CanadaFreePress.com*, March 9, 2005, http://www.canadafreepress.com/2005 /driessen030905.htm (August 18, 2009).

55. Annie Shattuck, "Global Food Security Act," *Foreign Policy in Focus*, April 17, 2009, http://www.fpif.org/fpiftxt/6050 (August 13, 2009).

55. Institute for Food and Development Policy, "Tell Congress Not to Force Genetically Engineered Crops on Other Countries as a Condition of Receiving Aid," *Food First Institute for Food and Development Policy*, May 19, 2009, http://www.foodfirst.org/en /node/2443 (August 13, 2009).

57. U.S. Food and Drug Administration, "Animal & Veterinary," *FDA*, July 1, 2009,

http://www.fda.gov/AnimalVeterinary/DevelopmentApprovalProcess /GeneticEngineering/GeneticallyEngineeredAnimals/ucm113605.htm (January 25, 2010).

56. Matthew Cossey, "The Baseless Campaign against GM Food," *Drum*, July 7, 2011, http://www.abc.net.au/unleashed/2785818.html (February 4, 2012).

53. British Broadcasting Corporation, "Charles in GM 'Disaster' Warning," *BBC News*, August 13, 2008, http://news.bbc.co.uk/2/hi/uk_news/7557644.stm (February 26, 2012).

60. Jeffrey Levi, Laura M. Segal, and Serena Vinter, *Keeping America's Food Safe: A Blueprint for Fixing the Food Safety System at the U.S. Department of Health and Human Services, Trust for America's Health*, March 2009, http://healthyamericans.org/assets /files/2009FoodSafetyReport.pdf (May 30, 2009).

62. Gardiner Harris, "U.S. Food Safety No Longer Improving," *New York Times*, April 10, 2009, A12.

65. Renee Johnson, *Japan's 2011 Earthquake and Tsunami: Food and Agriculture Implications* (Washington, DC: Congressional Research Service, April 13, 2011), summary.

59. U.S. Department of Health and Human Services, "Obama Administration Releases Food Safety Tips, New Report on Efforts to Protect Consumers from Foodborne Illness," *HHS.gov*, December 21, 2011, http://www.hhs.gov/news /press/2011pres/12/20111221a.html (February 26, 2012).

65. Aya Takada, "Japan's Food-Chain Treat Multiplies as Fukushima Radiation Spreads," *Bloomberg*, July 25, 2011, http://www.bloomberg.com/news/2011-07-24/threat-to-japanese-food-chain-multiplies-as-cesium-contamination-spreads.html (February 26, 2012).

68–69. Tom Alexander, "Conventional Agriculture Lobby Group Upset That White House Garden Is Going to Be Organic," *Growing Edge*, April 10, 2009, http://www .growingedge.com/chemical-fertilizer-group-upset-that-white-house-garden-is-going-to-be-organic (May 2, 2009).

68. Lisa Baertlein and Charles Abbott, "House Protects Pizza as a Vegetable," *Reuters*, November 18, 2011, http://www.reuters.com/article/2011/11/18/us-usa-lunch-idUSTRE7AH00020111118 (February 4, 2012).

70. Vershal Hogan, "Farm Subsidies More Than Welfare for Farmers," *Natchez Democrat*, February 21, 2010, http://www.natchezdemocrat.com/2010/02/21/farm-subsidies-more-than-welfare-for-farmers (February 26, 2012).

78. University of California Sustainable Agriculture Research and Education Program, "What Is Sustainable Agriculture?" *University of California Sustainable Agriculture Research and Education Program*, December 1997, http://www.sarep.ucdavis.edu /concept.htm (May 23, 2009).

82. United States Department of Agriculture, "Organic Production/Organic Food: Information Access Tools," *USDA*, December 10, 2008, http://www.nal.usda.gov /afsic/pubs/ofp/ofp.shtml (May 22, 2009).

83. Andrew Heintzman and Evan Solomon, eds., *Feeding the Future: From Fat to Famine, How to Solve the World's Food Crises* (Toronto: House of Anansi Press, 2004), 288.

83. Michael Pollan, "Why Bother," *New York Times Magazine*, April 20, 2008, http:// www.nytimes.com/2008/04/20/magazine/20wwln-lede-t.html?pagewanted=all (February 7, 2012).

SELECTED BIBLIOGRAPHY

Bergquist, Lee. "Taking Care of Cows' Business." *Milwaukee Journal Sentinel*, March 1, 2009. http://www.jsonline.com/news/wisconsin/40490387.html (April 26, 2011).

Bittman, Mark. "Rethinking the Meat-Guzzler." *New York Times*, January 27, 2008. http://www.nytimes.com/2008/01/27/weekinreview/27bittman.htm (May 29, 2011).

Bradsher, Keith. "A Drought in Australia, a Global Shortage of Rice." *New York Times*, April 17, 2008. http://www.nytimes.com/2008/04/17/business/worldbusiness/17warm.html?_r=1&hp&oref=slogin (February 22, 2011).

Brownell, Kelly D., and Katherine Battle Horgen. *Food Fight: The Inside Story of the Food Industry, America's Obesity Crisis, and What We Can Do about It*. Chicago: Contemporary Books, 2004.

Chin, Kimberley, and Kevin McGuire. "A Food Stamp Challenge That We All Can Help With. *Washington Post*, August 3, 2008, B08.

Congressional Research Service. "Labor Practices in the Meat Packing and Poultry Processing Industry: An Overview.*" National Agriculture Law Center*. October 27, 2006. http://www.nationalaglawcenter.org/assets/crs/RL33002.pdf (February 5, 2011).

Cook, Guy. *Genetically Modified Language*. New York: Routledge, 2005.

FAO, "Crisis in the Horn of Africa." *Food and Agriculture Organization of the United Nations*. 2012. http://www.fao.org/crisis/horn-africa/home/en (February 6, 2012).

Friedman, Thomas L. *Hot, Flat, and Crowded: Why We Need a Green Revolution—and How It Can Renew America*. New York: Farrar, Straus and Giroux, 2008.

Greenberg, Paul. *Four Fish: The Future of the Last Wild Food*. New York: Penguin, 2011.

Gurian-Sherman, Doug. *Failure to Yield: Evaluating the Performance of Genetically Engineered Crops*. Cambridge, MA: Union of Concerned Scientists, 2009.

Heintzman, Andrew, and Evan Solomon, eds. *Feeding the Future: From Fat to Famine, How to Solve the World's Food Crises*. Toronto: House of Anansi Press, 2006.

Human Rights Watch. "Blood, Sweat, and Fear." *Human Rights Watch*, January 24, 2005. http://www.hrw.org/en/node/11869/section/1 (February 6, 2011).

Ikerd, John. *Crisis and Opportunity: Sustainability in American Agriculture*. Lincoln, NE: Bison Books, 2008.

Imhoff, Daniel, ed. *CAFO: The Tragedy of Industrial Animal Factories*. San Rafael, CA: Earth Aware Editions, 2010.

International Fund for Agricultural Development. "Liquid Gold Helps Eritrean Farmers Defy the Looming Threat of Drought." *IFAD*. N.d. http://operations.ifad.org/web/guest/country/voice/tags/eritrea/eritreahoney# (May 16, 2011).

Lappe, Anna. *Diet for a Hot Planet: The Climate Crisis at the End of Your Fork and What You Can Do about It*. New York: Bloomsbury USA, 2010.

LeDuff, Charlie. "At a Slaughterhouse, Some Things Never Die." *New York Times*, June 16, 2000. http://www.nytimes.com/library/national/race/061600leduff-meat.html (February 17, 2011).

Live Science staff. "Staggering Amount of Food Wasted." *LiveScience.com*, May 14, 2008. http://www.livescience.com/health/080514-food-wasted.html (April 18, 2011).

Mann, Michael E., and Lee R. Kump. *Dire Predictions: Understanding Global Warming.* New York: Dorling Kindersley Books, 2008.

McGovern, George, Bob Dole, and Donald E. Messer. *Ending Hunger Now.* Minneapolis: Augsburg Fortress Publishers, 2005.

McKinley, Jesse. "Drought Adds to Hardships in California." *New York Times*, February 22, 2009. http://www.nytimes.com/2009/02/22/us/22mendota.html?_r=1&hp (February 22, 2011).

Morales, Alex. "Greenland and Antarctica Glaciers Speeding Faster Toward the Sea." *Bloomberg.com*, February 26, 2009. http://www.bloomberg.com/apps/news?pid=20601085 &sid=aTg9EF2NtBCg&refer=europe# (February 28, 2011).

Nestle, Marion. *Food Politics: How the Food Industry Influences Nutrition and Health.* Berkeley: University of California Press, 2002.

———. *What to Eat.* New York: North Point Press, 2006.

Paul, Helena, and Ricarda Steinbrecher. *Hungry Corporations: Transnational Biotech Companies Colonize the Food Chain.* London: Zed Books, 2003.

Petrini, Carlo. *Slow Food Nation: Why Our Food Should Be Good, Clean, and Fair.* New York: Rizzoli Ex Libris, 2007.

Pew Charitable Trusts and Johns Hopkins Bloomberg School of Public Health. *Putting Meat on the Table: Industrial Farm Animal Production in America.* Washington, DC: Pew Charitable Trusts and Johns Hopkins Bloomberg School of Public Health, 2008.

Pringle, Peter. *Food, Inc. Mendel to Monsanto—the Promises and Perils of the Biotech Harvest.* New York: Simon & Schuster, 2003.

Public Broadcasting Service. "Meatpacking in the U.S.: Still a 'Jungle' Out There?" *PBS*, December 15, 2006. http://www.pbs.org/now/shows/250/meat-packing.html (February 5, 2011).

Rhee, Foon. "Kerry Focuses Committee on Global Food Crisis." *Boston Globe*, March 24, 2009. http://www.boston.com/news/politics/politicalintelligence/2009/03/kerry_focuses_c.html (March 30, 2011).

Salatin, Joel. *Everything I Want to Do Is Illegal: War Stories from the Local Food Front.* Swoope, VA: Polyface Press, 2008.

Sullivan, Dan. "Agriculture and Climate Change." *Rodale Institute*, February 6, 2009. http://www.rodaleinstitute.org/20090206/gw1 (March 2, 2011).

Vegan Soapbox. "The Prevention of Farm Animal Cruelty Act: Pros & Cons." *Vegan Soapbox*, June 27, 2008. http://www.vegansoapbox.com/the-prevention-of-farm-animal-cruelty-act-pros-cons/ (February 5, 2011).

World Watch Institute. *State of the World 2009: Into a Warming World.* New York: W. W. Norton, 2009.

FURTHER INFORMATION

BOOKS

Fridell, Ron. *The War on Hunger*. Minneapolis: Twenty-First Century Books, 2003. This book discusses the many causes behind the world hunger crisis—including poverty, politics, and economics—and explains what people are doing to solve the problem.

Gay, Kathlyn. *Superfood or Superthreat: The Issue of Genetically Engineered Food*. Berkeley Heights, NJ: Enslow Publishers, 2008. Supporters say that genetically engineered food is the key to feeding a hungry world. Others say the harm to small farmers—and perhaps to human health—far outweigh the benefits. In this book, readers will learn about both sides of the controversy.

Johnson, Rebecca L. *Investigating Climate Change: Scientists Search for Answers in a Warming World*. Minneapolis: Twenty-First Century Books, 2009. This book tells readers not only why and how Earth is heating up but also how scientists study, measure, and track the phenomenon.

Kukathas, Uma. *The Global Food Crisis*. Farmington Hills, MI: Greenhaven Press, 2009. This anthology is presented in a pro-con format. Contributors debate whether capitalism has caused the world food crisis, whether the demand for biofuels is exacerbating the crisis, whether genetic engineering can solve the crisis, and other questions.

Kurlansky, Mark. *World without Fish*. New York: Workman Publishing Company, 2011. In this full-color graphic novel, Kurlansky and illustrator Frank Stockton examine threats to the world's oceans and the fish that live there. The book explores overfishing, water pollution, and the harmful effects of climate change on ocean life. It also tells what kids can do to support sustainable fishing and cleaner oceans.

Owen, Marna. *Animal Rights: Noble Cause or Needless Effort?* Minneapolis: Twenty-First Century Books, 2010. The fair and humane treatment of animals is a key issue in the debate over agricultural practices and the production of fashionable clothing and makeup. This title, organized in a pro/con format, is part of the USA TODAY's Debate series, offering a range of voices and perspectives on issues of concern in the twenty-first century.

Pollan, Michael. *The Omnivore's Dilemma for Kids: The Secrets behind What You Eat*. New York: Dial, 2009. Here, Pollan has revised his best-selling adult book for a younger audience. Readers will learn about the hazards of industrialized farming, the benefits of organic farming, and the need for sustainable agricultural practices.

Roberts, Jack L. *Organic Agriculture: Protecting Our Food Supply or Chasing Imaginary Risks?* Minneapolis: Twenty-First Century Books, 2012. This title is organized in a pro/con format to discuss the arguments for and against organic farming practices. The title is part of the USA TODAY's Debate series, offering a range of voices and perspectives on issues of concern in the twenty-first century.

Tagliaferro, Linda. *Genetic Engineering*. Minneapolis: Twenty-First Century Books, 2010. Some people say that genetic engineering can help us wipe out world hunger, disease, and other problems. But critics say that genetic engineering has many downsides. The title is part of the USA TODAY's Debate series, offering a range of voices and perspectives on issues of concern in the twenty-first century.

FILMS

Food, Inc. DVD. New York: Magnolia Home Entertainment, 2009.
This film examines the industrialized U.S. food system and shows how multinational corporations have taken over food production. It shows the effects of industrialized food production on animal welfare, the environment, human health, the economy, and workers' rights.

The Future of Food. DVD. Mill Valley, CA: Lily Films, 2004.
This documentary investigates genetically engineered foods and the cost of a global food system that pushes farmers off the land.

An Inconvenient Truth. DVD. Los Angeles: Paramount Pictures, 2006.
Featuring former U.S. vice president Al Gore, this documentary film examines climate change, how it might affect Earth and human society, and what people can do to reverse the damage.

Six Degrees Could Change the World. VHS. Washington, DC: National Geographic, 2008.
This documentary film explores what could happen to Earth if global warming increases by 1°, then 2°, and up to 6°C (1.8°, 3.6°, and 10.8°F) by the year 2100. The film also shows how global warming has already affected Australia, Greenland, and the Amazonian rain forest of South America.

WEBSITES

AgBioWorld
http://www.agbioworld.org
AgBioWorld believes that genetic engineering of food crops (agricultural biotechnology) offers many benefits and few risks for consumers. The group's website provides extensive information on agricultural biotechnology.

CAFO: The Tragedy of Industrial Animal Factories
http://www.cafothebook.org
This website, a companion to the book of the same name, offers details on the inhumane practices of industrial food production, explains what consumers can do to stop factory farming, and offers links to numerous other resources.

Friends of the Earth
http://www.foe.org
Friends of the Earth is an environmental protection organization. Its website offers information on global warming, genetic engineering, pollution, and more.

International Food Policy Research Institute (IFPRI)
http://www.ifpri.org
The IFPRI seeks sustainable solutions for ending hunger and poverty. It works around the world to provide nutritious food to hungry people and to support sustainable agriculture. The IFPRI website describes its goals and programs.

Michael Pollan
http://www.michaelpollan.com
Michael Pollan's best-selling books include *In Defense of Food* and *The Omnivore's Dilemma.* His website includes articles on a variety of food topics, including animal welfare, farm policy, food safety, GE foods, nutrition, organic foods, and sustainable agriculture.

Slow Food International
http://www.slowfood.com/
Slow Food was founded in 1989 to counter the rise of fast food and fast life, the disappearance of local food traditions, and people's dwindling interest in the food they eat. The group's website describes the slow food philosophy and what consumers can do to support small-scale and sustainable food production.

Union of Concerned Scientists
http://www.ucsusa.org/
The Union of Concerned Scientists is a science-based nonprofit organization working for a healthy environment and a safer world. Its website offers articles on food and agriculture, global warming, clean energy, and other topics.

World Food Programme
http://www.wfp.org
Part of the United Nations, the World Food Programme is the largest humanitarian organization fighting hunger worldwide. The group's website gives a country-by-country breakdown of its activities around the world. It also offers statistics, articles, and up-to-date news about the fight against world hunger.

INDEX

ABOUT THE AUTHOR

Kathlyn Gay is the author of more than one hundred nonfiction books on a variety of topics, including social issues, environmental preservation, history (U.S., Russian, and Chinese), health, religious and cultural diversity, food security, and eating disorders. She has also written teacher manuals, ESL programs, portions of textbooks, and reference works. She has been featured in *The World's Who's Who of Authors, Contemporary Authors, About the Author,* and *Junior Authors and Illustrators.* Some of her titles for Twenty-First Century Books include *The Aftermath of the Russian Revolution, The Aftermath of the Chinese Nationalist Revolution,* and *Mao Zedong's China.*

PHOTO ACKNOWLEDGMENTS

The images in this book are used with the permission of: AP Photo/Kevin Frayer, pp. 2–3, 12, 19 (bottom), 44, 72; © Daniel Berehulak/Getty Images, pp. 4–5; © Laura Westlund/Independent Picture Service, pp. 6–7, 41, 71; REUTERS/Eduardo Munoz, p. 7; © G.M.B. Akash/Panos Pictures, pp. 8–9; © Will Vragovic/St. Petersburg Times/ZUMA Press/CORBIS, p. 11 (top); © Robin Nelson/Zuma Press/CORBIS, p. 11 (bottom); AP Photo/Intelligencer Journal, Richard Hertzler, p. 13; AP Photo/Reed Saxon, p. 15; © Hulton Archive/Getty Images, pp. 16–17; REUTERS/Ed Harris, p. 19 (top); © Stephen Coddington/St. Petersburg Times/ZUMA Press/Newscom, p. 21; © Daniel Pepper/Getty Images, p. 22; © Animals Animals/SuperStock, pp. 24–25; © Kevin Moloney/Aurora Photos/CORBIS, p. 27; © Mitch Kezar/AgStock Images/CORBIS, p. 29; © Wojciech Grzedzinski for The International Herald Tribune/Redux, p. 32; AP Photo, p. 33; © J. Emilio Flores/CORBIS, p. 34 (top); © Paul Grebliunas/Stone/Getty Images, p. 34 (bottom); © Todd Strand/Independent Picture Service, p. 37; AP Photo/Khalil Senosi, pp. 38–39; © age fotostock/SuperStock, pp. 42–43; © Scott Olson/Getty Images, p. 45; © Dario Pignatelli/Bloomberg/Getty Images, p. 46; © Joerg Boethling/Alamy, pp. 48–49; © Universal Pictures/MoviePix/Hulton Archive/Getty Images, p. 50; © Paulo Fridman/Bloomberg/Getty Images, pp. 52–53; © Khaled Desouki/AFP/Getty Images, p. 54; © Barrett & MacKay Photo, p. 57; © Dr. Gary Gaugler/Visuals Unlimited, Inc., pp. 58–59; AP Photo/Elaine Thompson, p. 61; Imaginechina via AP Images, p. 63; © Ko Sasaki/The New York Times/Redux, p. 65; © Yellow Dog Productions/The Image Bank/Getty Images, pp. 66–67; AP Photo/Alex Brandon, pp. 68–69; AP Photo/Mohamed Sheikh Nor, p. 73; © Tariq Mahmood/AFP/Getty Images, p. 74; © Huw Jones/Photolibrary/Getty Images, pp. 76–77; © Catherine Karnow/CORBIS, p. 78; © Nigel Cattlin/Visuals Unlimited, Inc., p. 79; AP Photo/The Daily News-Record, Holly Marcus, p. 80; © Virginie Montet/AFP/Getty Images, p. 82.

Front cover: © Arco Images GmbH/Alamy.
Back cover: AP Photo/Kevin Frayer.

DISCARDED BY
FREEPORT
MEMORIAL LIBRARY

YOUNG ADULT

FREEPORT MEMORIAL LIBRARY